THE ALBATROSS
MODERN CONTINENTAL LIBRARY
VOLUME 52

*

JOURNAL OF
KATHERINE MANSFIELD

KU-732-311

THE ALBATROSS MODERN CONTINENTAL LIBRARY
includes the following works by
KATHERINE MANSFIELD

*

JOURNAL
of
KATHERINE MANSFIELD

Edited by

J. MIDDLETON MURRY

THE ALBATROSS
HAMBURG · PARIS · BOLOGNA

TO
MARY ARDEN

COPYRIGHT 1933
BY THE ALBATROSS VERLAG G. M. B. H., HAMBURG
IMPRIMÉ EN ALLEMAGNE

CONTENTS

INTRODUCTION

KATHERINE MANSFIELD (KATHERINE MIDDLE-
ton Murry, *née* Kathleen Beauchamp) was born in Wellington, New Zealand, on October 14, 1888. She was the
third daughter of a family of five. The Beauchamps had
been in Australia and New Zealand for three generations. The greater part of her early childhood was spent
in a small township called Karori, a few miles from
Wellington, where the village school was the only
school, and where she shared what education there was
with the milk boy and the washerwoman's daughters
(see 'The Doll's House'). She has left it on record that
she had her first story accepted at the age of nine—I
remember her saying that it appeared in a magazine
called *The Lone Hand*—and that, at the same age, she
gained the first prize for English composition at the
village school, the subject being 'A Sea Voyage'.

At the age of thirteen she was sent to be educated
in England, at Queen's College, Harley Street, where
she remained till eighteen. There she edited the college
magazine. Like other young people of her generation,
she found the beginning of intellectual freedom through
an admiration of Oscar Wilde and the English 'decad-
ents', but, at this time, her main interests shifted over
from literature to music. She became a devotee of the
violoncello, and a fine executant.

She returned to New Zealand much against her will,
and spent the next two years of her life in fairly constant
rebellion against what she then considered the narrow-

ness and provincialism of a remote colonial city. Inevitably, London appeared to her as the living centre of all artistic and intellectual life. A family of musicians in Wellington, whom she knew intimately, and who had been a kind of oasis for her in what seemed to her an intellectual desert, left New Zealand for London. At their departure she was in despair. She went on a rough camping expedition through the New Zealand bush. On her return she persuaded her parents to allow her to return to London on a small allowance.

Shortly afterwards, she finally abandoned music for literature. She submitted manuscripts to editors in vain, and, in her effort to make ends meet, she had varied and exacting experiences in minor parts in travelling opera companies and the like, until the quality of her writing was recognized by the editor of *The New Age*. From 1909 to 1911 she was a fairly constant contributor to that paper. A series of stories she wrote for *The New Age*, based upon her experiences while convalescent in Germany after an illness, was collected and published in 1911, under the title *In a German Pension*. This book was immediately recognized. It passed quickly into three editions, when its sale was disastrously interrupted by the sudden bankruptcy of her publisher. For *In a German Pension* she received £15 in advance of royalties, of which, of course, there were none.

In December 1911 I met her at the house of the late W. L. George, the novelist. I was, at that time, an Oxford undergraduate, editing together with Michael

Sadleir a youthful literary magazine called *Rhythm*. Katherine Mansfield began to write stories regularly for this. Her first story, 'The Woman at the Store', caused a minor sensation. *Rhythm*, which became for its last three numbers *The Blue Review*, lasted for about a year longer, during most of which Katherine Mansfield and I edited it together. Most of the stories she contributed to it, sometimes two a month, have been republished in *Something Childish, and other Stories*.

When *The Blue Review* died, in July 1913, Katherine Mansfield had no place to write in. The beautiful story, *Something Childish but very Natural*, which she wrote in Paris in December 1913, was refused by every editor to whom she submitted it. No home could be found for any one of her stories till the winter of 1915, when she and D. H. Lawrence and I produced three numbers of a little magazine called *The Signature*, written wholly by ourselves. *The Signature* died within two months, and again Katherine Mansfield had nowhere to write, until I became editor of *The Athenæum* in 1919. In the four years between 1915 and 1919, three stories of hers were published by English periodicals, all in 1918. 'Bliss' in *The English Review*, and 'Pictures' and 'The Man Without a Temperament' in *Art and Letters*. In 1917, however, *Prelude* had been published as a little blue-paper book by the Hogarth Press, and in 1918 *Je ne parle pas français* was printed for private circulation by my brother and myself.

Prelude marks the beginning of the final phase in

INTRODUCTION

Katherine Mansfield's development. The war had come as a profound spiritual shock to her, as it did to many less gifted writers of her generation. For a long period the chaos into which her thoughts and ideals and purposes had been flung remained unresolved. Then slowly her mind began to turn back towards her early childhood as a life which had existed apart from, and uncontaminated by, the mechanical civilization which had produced the war. The crucial moment was when, in 1915, her dearly loved younger brother arrived in England to serve as an officer. Her meeting with him formed, as it were, a point round which her changed attitude could crystallize. They talked over their early childhood for hours on end, and Katherine Mansfield resolved to dedicate herself to recreating life as she had lived and felt it in New Zealand. Her brother's death a month later confirmed her in her purpose, and shortly afterwards she left England for Bandol in the south of France, and began to work on a long story of her childhood days called *The Aloe*, which was published in a different and shortened form as *Prelude*.

On its appearance as a blue-paper volume *Prelude* was completely ignored. Most of the newspapers to which it was sent did not review it at all. The two which did saw nothing particular in it. But Katherine Mansfield had her moment of triumph when she heard that the local printer who set up the book had exclaimed on reading the MS., 'My! but these kids are *real!*' It was characteristic of her that she preferred the praise of simple, 'unliterary' people to that of the cultured and the critics; and this characteristic became still more marked later on, when, after the publication of *Bliss*, she began to receive many letters from simple people who loved her work, and, above all, the child Kezia who appeared in it. She felt she had a responsibility to these people. To them she must tell the truth, and nothing but the truth. This preoccupation with truth, in what she told and in herself to be worthy to tell it, became the devouring passion of her last years. She turned away from modern literature: so little of contemporary work seemed to her to be 'true'. 'The writers are not *humble*,' she used to say; they were not serving the great purpose which literature exists to serve.

In the meantime *Prelude* was hardly more than a *succès d'estime*, if indeed it was that. Not until it appeared as the first story in *Bliss* was its unique and exquisitely original quality truly appreciated.

But in December 1917, just after she had finished revising the MS. of *Prelude* for the printer, Katherine Mansfield had a serious attack of pleurisy. The gloom and depression and sunlessness of a London now completely under the shadow of the war had a profound effect on one whose childhood had been spent in a gentler air. She pined for the sun; she was confident that she had only to revisit her beloved Bandol in the south of France to be well again. Accordingly she left England at the beginning of January 1918. But travelling conditions in France in the last year of the war were such that the hardships she suffered on the journey (which she had to undertake alone) made her illness worse, and to her dismay, Bandol itself was utterly changed; it also had been wasted by the war. No sooner had she reached the place, ill and alone, than she passionately desired to return to England. Tragic ill-fortune dogged her efforts to return. The authorities delayed for weeks before granting their permission; and on the very day she arrived in Paris, weak and by this time very seriously ill, the long-range bombardment of Paris began, and all civilian traffic between England and France was suspended. The hardships of her journey in France turned her pleurisy into consumption.

She went to Looe in Cornwall for the summer of 1918, and returned to a new house in Hampstead for the winter. In the spring of 1919 I became editor of *The Athenæum*, and she began to write weekly criticisms of novels under the initials K.M., which then began to be famous, and a little later began to write a story each month for the paper. Then, for the first time, the publishers began to ask her to collect her stories, and at the beginning of 1920 *Bliss*, for which she received £40 in advance, appeared.

Before it appeared, she had been driven from England once more by her illness. She spent the winter of 1919-1920 in Ospedaletti and Mentone, where she learned of the success of her book. She returned to

Hampstead for the summer, and in September left once more for Mentone. From Mentone she went, in May 1921, to Montana in Switzerland.

In the autumn of 1921 she completed *The Garden Party, and Other Stories*, which was published in the spring of 1922, while she was in Paris whither she had gone for a special treatment in February. The appearance of *The Garden Party* finally established her as the most remarkable short-story writer of her generation in England.

But now in 1922 writing had become for her an almost impossible struggle, not only against disease, but against an inward conviction that some work of inward purification had to be accomplished before she could go forward, before she would be worthy to express the complete truth which in her imagination she apprehended. *The Canary*, the last complete story she wrote, was completed in July 1922. In the October following she deliberately abandoned writing for the time and went into retirement at Fontainebleau, where she died suddenly and unexpectedly on the night of January 9, 1923.

It is difficult for me to attempt a critical valuation of Katherine Mansfield's work. For years I was involved in it. I believed in it, published it, and for one brief moment even printed it with my own hands. And now, and always, it is and will be impossible for me to be wholly detached from it. I can only say that her work seems to me to be of a finer and purer kind than that of her contemporaries. It is more spontaneous, more vivid, more delicate and more beautiful. Katherine Mansfield responded more completely to life than any writer I have known, and the effect of that more complete response is in her work.

Her affinities are rather with the English poets than the English prose-writers. There is no English prose-writer to whom she can be related.[1] The revolution which she made in the art of short story in England was altogether personal. Many writers have attempted to carry on her work; not one has come within a measurable distance of success. Her secret died with her. And of the many critics who have tried to define the quality in her work which makes it so inimitable, every one has been compelled to give up the attempt in despair. It is noticeable, however, that the most whole-hearted admiration her work has received comes pre-eminently from the most distinguished short-story writers we have in England—H. G. Wells, John Galsworthy, Walter de la Mare, H. M. Tomlinson, Stacy

[1] There is a certain resemblance between Katherine Mansfield's stories and those of Anton Tchehov. But this resemblance is often exaggerated by critics, who seem to believe that Katherine Mansfield learned her art from Tchehov. That is a singularly superficial view of the relation, which was one of kindred temperaments. In fact, Katherine Mansfield's technique is very different from Tchehov's. She admired and understood Tchehov's work as few English writers have done; she had (as her *Journal* shows) a deep personal affection for the man, whom, of course, she never knew. But her method was wholly her own, and her development would have been precisely the same had Tchehov never existed.

Aumonier, Barry Pain, Ethel Colburn Mayne. These practitioners of the art, with one voice, salute her as *hors concours*, though they find it as difficult as any critic to say wherein her superiority consists. And perhaps a more remarkable fact is that her stories have met with an unusual popular success. For all her art, perhaps more truly because her art was of a peculiarly instinctive kind, Katherine Mansfield's stories are read and loved by innumerable simple people, who find in her characters a living reality which is rare in the literature they read. And it may be that the simplest criticism of her work is the truest; and that the most adequate judgement upon her writing is that of the printer whom I have quoted: 'But these kids are *real!*'

It is, however, impossible for one who knew her intimately, who (in a sense) worked with her during the greater part of her career as a writer, who copied and punctuated and criticized her stories as they were written, to be silent on one element in her nature which, it seems to me, was essential to a peculiar quality of her work. This peculiar quality of her work I can only describe as a kind of *purity*. It is as though the glass through which she looked upon life were crystal-clear. And this quality of her work corresponds to a quality in her life. Katherine Mansfield was natural and spontaneous as was no other human being I have ever met. She seemed to adjust herself to life as a flower adjusts itself to the earth and to the sun. She suffered greatly, she delighted greatly: but her suffering and her delight were never partial, they filled the whole of her. She was utterly generous, utterly courageous; when she gave herself, to life, to love, to some spirit of truth which she served, she gave royally. She loved life—with all its beauty and its pain; she accepted life completely, and she had the right to accept it, for she had endured in herself all the suffering which life can lavish upon a single soul.

The brief biographical sketch printed above was written for the information of the many people who have asked me for particulars of Katherine Mansfield's life. It is printed here to serve as a background to the Journal and the two volumes of letters now in preparation. As for the Journal itself, a few words of introduction are necessary.

At various times in her life Katherine Mansfield entertained the plan of writing for publication 'a kind of minute note-book' (see the entry of January 22, 1916). Three separate attempts to carry the plan into execution can be traced in her manuscripts, and once she got so far as to tell me to arrange with a publisher for its publication. The notes for this 'note-book' would have been rewritten from entries in her Journal. In a few cases, as in May 1919, the original Journal entry and the note exist side by side.

The remaining material of which the Journal is composed is of various kinds—brief (and sometimes difficult) notes for stories, fragments of diaries, unposted letters, comments and confessions scattered through her manuscripts. To these I have added a minimum of necessary words of explanation.

Save for a single entry the Journal begins in 1914. The 'huge complaining diaries' of which Katherine Mansfield speaks (February 14, 1916) were all destroyed. She was ruthless with her own past, and I have little doubt that what has survived is almost wholly that which, for one reason or another, she wished to survive.

JOHN MIDDLETON MURRY.

JOURNAL

1910

[K.M. ruthlessly destroyed all record of the time between her return from New Zealand to England in 1909, and 1914. The following fragment is all that remains of her 'huge complaining diaries' (see p. 64). It belongs to 1910, to that stay in Bavaria which was the origin of her first book, *In a German Pension*. A subsequent allusion to her misery in Bavaria will be found in her Journal of December 1920.]

JUNE [1910]. IT IS AT LAST OVER, THIS WEARISOME day, and dusk is beginning to sift in among the branches of the drenched chestnut tree. I think I must have caught cold in my beautiful exultant walk yesterday, for to-day I am ill. I began to work but could not. Fancy wearing two pairs of stockings and two coats and a hot-water bottle in June, and shivering. . . . I think it is the pain that makes me shiver and feel dizzy. To be alone all day, in a house whose every sound seems foreign to you, and to feel a terrible confusion in your body which affects you mentally, suddenly pictures for you detestable incidents, revolting personalities, which you only shake off to find recurring again as the pain seems to grow worse again. Alas! I shall not walk with bare feet in wild woods again. Not until I have grown accustomed to the climate. . . .

The only adorable thing I can imagine is for my Grandmother to put me to bed and bring me a bowl of hot bread and milk, and, standing with her hands folded, the left thumb over the right, say in her adorable voice: 'There, darling, isn't that nice?' Oh, what a miracle of happiness that would be. To wake later to find her turning down the bedclothes to see if my feet were cold, and wrapping them up in a little pink singlet, softer than cat's fur. . . . Alas!

Sunday Morning. Yet another Sunday. . . . It is raining again to-day—just a steady persistent rain that seems to drift one from one morning to the other. When I had finished writing I went down to supper, drank a little soup, and the old Doctor next me suddenly said: 'Please go to bed *now*,' and I went like a lamb and drank some hot milk. It was a night of agony. When I felt morning was at last come, I lighted a candle, looked at the watch, and found it was just a quarter to twelve! Now I know what it is to fight a drug. Veronal was on the table by my bed. Oblivion—deep sleep—think of it! But I didn't take any. Now I am up and dressed. . . .

1914

[In February 1914, when the following entries were made, Katherine Mansfield and I were living in Paris, at 32 rue de Tournon. We found it impossible to earn enough money, and I had to return to London to look for work.]

'A CALM, IRRESISTIBLE WELL-BEING—ALMOST mystic in character, and yet doubtless connected with physical conditions' [*Dorothy Wordsworth's Journal*].
 Writes Dorothy:

> William (P.G.) is very well,
> And gravely blithe—you know his way—
> Talking with woodruff and harebell
> And idling all the summer day
> As he can well afford to do.
> (P.G. for that again.) For who
> Is more Divinely Entitled to?
> He rises and breakfasts sharp at seven,
> Then pastes some fern-fronds in his book,
> Until his milk comes at eleven
> With two fresh scones baked by the cook.
> And then he paces in the sun
> Until we dine at half past one.
> 'God and the cook are very good,'
> Laughs William, relishing his food.
> (Sometimes the tears rush to my eyes:
> How kind he is, and oh, how wise!)
> After, he sits and reads to me
> Until at four we take our tea.
> My dear, you hardly would believe
> That William could so sigh and grieve
> Over a simple, childish tale
> How 'Mary trod upon the Snail',

Or 'Little Ernie lost his Pail'.
And then perhaps a good half-mile
He walks to get an appetite
For supper, which we take at night
In the substantial country style.
By nine he's in bed and fast asleep,
Not *snoring*, dear, but very deep,
Oh, very deep asleep indeed. . . .

And so on *ad lib*. What a Pa man!

I am going to read Goethe. Except for a few poems, I know nothing of his well. I shall read 'Poetry and Truth' immediately.

'When all is done human life is at its greatest and best but a little froward child to be played with, and humoured a little, to keep it quiet until it falls asleep, and then the care is over' (Temple).

That's the sort of strain—not for what it says and means, but for the 'lilt' of it—that sets me writing.

The Child in my Arms.

'Will you touch me with the child in my arms?' is no mere pleasantry. Change the 'will' into 'can' and it's *tief, sehr tief!* I was thinking just now . . . that I hardly dare give rein to my thoughts of J. and my longing for J. And I thought: if I had a child, I would play with it now and *lose myself in it* and kiss it and make it laugh. And I'd use a child as my guard against my deepest feeling.

When I felt: 'No, I'll think no more of this; it's intolerable and unbearable,' I'd dance the baby.

That's true, I think, of all, all women. And it accounts for the curious look of security that you see in young mothers: they are safe from any *ultimate* state of feeling because of the child in their arms. And it accounts also for the women who call men 'children'. Such women fill themselves with their men—gorge themselves really into a state of absolute heartlessness. Watch the sly, satisfied smile of women who say, 'Men are nothing but babies!'

'They were neither of them quite enough in love to imagine that £350 a year would supply them with all the comforts of life' (Jane Austen's 'Elinor and Edward'). My God! say I.

I went to J.'s room and looked through the window. It was evening, with little light, and what was there was very soft—the Freak Hour when people never seem to be quite in focus. I watched a man walking up and down the road—and he looked like a fly walking up a wall—and some men straining up with a barrow—all bottoms and feet. In the house opposite, at a ground-floor window, heavily barred, sat a little dark girl in a grey shawl reading a book. Her hair was parted down the middle: she had a small, oval face. She was perfectly charming, so set in the window with the shining white of the book. I felt a sort of Spanish infatuation. . . .

It is as though God opened his hand and let you dance on it a little, and then shut it up tight—so tight that you could not even cry. . . . The wind is terrible to-night. I am very tired—but I can't go to bed. I can't *sleep* or *eat*. Too tired.

'It was the touch of art that P. was suffering, the inexorable magic touch that still transforms in spite of us; that never hesitates to test and examine the materials it has to transmute, but never fails to transmute them.'

[By the end of February 1914 we had returned to London, with very little but the clothes we stood in. For a few weeks we lived in a furnished flat in Beaufort Mansions, Chelsea. From the back windows one had a view of a timber-yard and a cemetery.]

A Dream.

March 6. K.T. and her sister were walking down a road that was bounded on one side by a high hill and had on the other a deep ravine. So deep was the ravine that the cliffs at its base shone like points of teeth, sharp and tiny. Her sister was very frightened and clung to her arm, trembling and crying. So K.T. hid her terror and said, 'It is all right. It is perfectly all right.' She had a little black fur muff slipped over one hand.

Suddenly there came driving towards them a chariot like the one in her Latin book, drawn by six stumpy horses and driven by a charioteer in a skull-cap. They came at a furious gallop, but the charioteer was calm; a quiet evil smile dyed his lips.

'Oh, K.T.! Oh, K.T.! I'm frightened,' sobbed her sister.

'It's quite all right. It's perfectly all right,' scolded K.T.

But as she watched the chariot a strange thing took place. Though the horses maintained their tearing gallop, they were not coming towards her and her sister, *but were galloping backwards*, while the charioteer smiled as though with deep satisfaction. K.T. put her little black muff over her sister's face. 'They're gone. They're quite gone.' But now the deafening clatter came from behind them like the sound of an army of horsemen in clashing armour. Louder and louder and nearer and nearer came the noise. 'Oh, K.T.! Oh, K.T.!' moaned her sister and K.T. shut her lips, only pressing her sister's arm. The noise was upon them—in a moment—*now*.

And nothing passed but a black horse as tall as a house with a dark serene rider in a wide hat gliding past them like a ship through dark water, and gliding importantly down the hill. The sight was so fearful that K.T. knew she dreamed. 'I must wake up at once.' And she made every effort to shut her eyes and shake away the scene, but it would not go. She tried to call and she felt her lips open, but no sound would come. She shouted and screamed without a sound until at last she felt her bed and lifted her head into the burning dark of the bedroom.

The view from my window this morning is so tremendously exciting. A high wind is blowing and the glass is dashed with rain. In the timber-yard beside the cemetery there are large pools of water, and smoke blows from . . .

March 19. Dreamed about New Zealand. Very delightful.

March 20. Dreamed about N.Z. again—one of the painful dreams when I'm there and hazy about my return ticket.

March 21. Travelled with two brown women. One had a basket of chickweed on her arm, the other a basket of daffodils. They both carried babies bound, somehow, to them with a torn shawl. Neat spare women with combed and braided hair. They slung talk at each other across the bus. Then one woman took a piece of bread from her sagging pocket and gave it to the baby, the other opened her bodice and put the child to her breast. They sat and rocked their knees and darted their quick eyes over the bus load. Busy and indifferent they looked.

March 22. Went to the Albert Hall with B.C. A bad, dull concert. But I thought all the while that I'd rather be with musical people than any others, and that they're mine, really. A violinist (miles away) bent his head and his hair grew like G.'s: that made me think so, I suppose. I ought to be able to write about them wonderfully.

March 23. When I get by myself, I am always more or less actively miserable. If it were not for J. I should live quite alone. It's raining; I have a cold and my fire has gone out. Sparrows outside are cheeping like chickens. Oh heavens! what a different scene the sound recalls! The warm sun, and the tiny yellow balls, so dainty, treading down the grass blades, and Sheehan giving me the smallest chick wrapped in a flannel to carry to the kitchen fire. [Sheehan was the original of Pat in *Prelude*.]

March 24. Mother's birthday. I wrote at 2 o'clock and got up and sat on the box of the window thinking of her. I would love to see her again and the little frown between her brows, and to hear her voice. But I don't think I will. My memory of her is so complete that I don't think it will be disturbed. [It was not; Katherine Mansfield did not see her mother again.]

The P.'s dined with us last night. It was dull. They are worthy and pleasant, but Mrs. P. is a weight, and P. makes me feel old. He only likes me because of what I used to be like, and he thinks the 'normal' me abnormally quiet and a bit lifeless. I don't want to see them again. Thank God! there's a sprinkle of sun to-day.

The river to-night was low and the little walls and

towers and chimneys on the opposite bank black against the night. I keep thinking of *Paris* and *money*. I am getting all *my* spring out of the sunsets.

March 25. L.M. and I travelled miles to-day. We sat in a bus talking, and now and again when I looked up, I kept seeing the squares with their butterfly leaves just ready to fly. We met near the old haunts—Queen Anne Street—and walked in one of the little lanes and short cuts that we know so well—side by side, talking. 'Let me tie your veil,' and I stop; she ties it and we walk on again. In the Persian shop she leaned against a red and black silk curtain. She was very pale, and her black hat looked enormous, and she kept wanting to buy me 'these things—feel how soft they are,' and smiling and speaking just above her breath for tiredness.

March 26. New Moon, 6h. 9m. p.m. (I didn't see it, though). L.M. and I took the tram to Clapham. She left at about 9 p.m. having dressed me. When I leave her hands I feel hung with wreaths. A silly, unreal evening at Miss R.'s. Pretty rooms and pretty people, pretty coffee, and cigarettes out of a silver tankard. A sort of sham Meredith atmosphere lurking. A.R. has a pert, nice face—that was all. I was wretched. I have nothing to say to 'charming' women. I feel like a cat among tigers. The ladies, left to themselves, talked ghosts and child-beds. I am wretchedly unhappy among everybody—and the silence . . .

March 27. I am writing for L.M. to come. She's very late. Everything is in a state of suspense—even birds and chimneys. Frightened *in private*.

At the last moment L.M. never said Good-bye at all but took the fiddle and ran. I walked away down some narrow streets; large drops of rain fell. I passed some packing warehouses, and the delicious smell of fresh wood and straw reminded me of Wellington. I could almost fancy a saw-mill. In the evening the C.'s, and the little parrot swinging on a wire.

March 28. Put my clothes in order. The crocuses in Battersea reminded me of autumn in Bavaria. The ground is wet, and it looks as though winter were going —the grass long and green among the trampled flowers. Birds are far more savage-looking than the wildest beasts. Thinking of a forest of *wild* birds—or if the birds 'turned' even here. I want to get alone. The *magnolia conspicua* is in bud.

March 29. I am going to start a play to-day.

March 30. 'I am afraid you are too psychological, Mr. Temple.' Then I went off and bought the bacon.

March 31. A splendid fine morning, but as I know I have to go out and change the cheque and pay the bills, I can do nothing and I feel wretched. Life is a hateful business, there's no denying it. When G. and J. were talking in the Park of physical well-being and of how they could still look forward to 'parties', I nearly groaned. And I am sure J. could get a great deal of pleasure out of pleasant society. I couldn't. I've done with it, and can't combat it at all now. I had so much rather lean idly over the bridge and watch the boats and the free, unfamiliar people and feel the wind blow. No, I hate society. The idea of the play seems perfect tripe to-day.

April 1. Spent another frightful day. Nothing helps or could help me except a person who could guess. Went for a walk and had some vague comfort given by some children and the noise of the water like rising waves.

April 2. I have begun to sleep badly again and I've decided to tear up everything that I've written and start again. I'm sure that is best. This misery persists, and I am so crushed under it. If I could write with my old fluency for *one day*, the spell would be broken. It's the continual effort—the slow building-up of my idea and then, before my eyes and out of my power, its slow dissolving.

April 3. Went for a walk by the river this evening and watched the boats. Two had red sails and one had white. The trees are budding almost before one's eyes in this warm weather—big white buds like birds on the chestnut trees, and round trees just sprinkled with green. The

world is exceedingly lovely. My letter to L.M. was a
great effort. She seemed somehow 'out of the running'.
But then so does everybody. I feel a real horror of people
closing over me. I could not *bear* them. I wish I lived
on a barge, with J. for a husband and a little boy for
a son.

April 4. Won a moral victory this morning, to my great
relief. Went out to spend 2s. 11d. and left it unspent.
But I have never known a more hideous day. Terribly
lonely. Nothing that isn't satirical is really true for me
to write just now. If I try to find things lovely, I turn
pretty-pretty. And at the same time I am so frightened
of writing mockery for satire that my pen hovers and
won't settle. Dined with C.'s and D. Afterwards to
Café Royal. The sheep were bleating and we set up a
feeble counterpart. Saw a fight. The woman with her
back to me—her arms crooked sharp at the elbows, her
head thrust out, like a big bird.

April 5. No bird sits a tree more proudly than a
pigeon. It looks as though placed there by the Lord.
The sky was silky blue and white, and the sun shone
through the little leaves. But the children, pinched
and crooked, made me feel a bit out of love with God.

April 6. I went out with J. to find a shop; but instead
we came to Swan Walk and passed and repassed and
remarked the delightful houses, white with flowering

pear-trees in the gardens and green railings and fine carved gates. I want a little house very much. My mind is full of embroidery, but there isn't any material to hold it together or make it strong. A silly state! L.M. seems to be simply fading away. I can barely remember her objectively: subjectively she is just the same.

April 7. The heavens opened for the sunset to-night. When I had thought the day folded and sealed, came a burst of heavenly bright petals. . . . I sat behind the window, pricked with rain, and looked until that hard thing in my breast melted and broke into the smallest fountain, murmuring as aforetime, and I drank the sky and the whisper. Now who is to decide between 'Let it be' and 'Force it'? J. believes in the whip: he says his steed has plenty of strength, but it is idle and shies at such a journey in prospect. I feel, if mine does not gallop and dance at free will, I am not riding at all, but just swinging from its tail. For example, to-day. . . . To-night he's all sparks.

May. To-day is Sunday. It is raining a little, and the birds are cheeping. There's a smell of food and a noise of chopping cabbage.

Oh, if only I could make a celebration and do a bit of writing. I long and long to write, and the words just won't come. It's a queer business. Yet, when I read people like Gorky, for instance, I realize how streets ahead of them I be. . . .

July. . . . Then I put my hand over it and felt for a latch, and then through the bars. I suppose one isn't expected to vault over it, I thought—or to ride a bicycle up this side and dive into a fountain of real water on the other. . . .

To Beauty. Why should you come to-night when it is so cold and grey and when the clouds are heavy and the bees troubled in their swinging?

August 17. I simply cannot believe that there was a time when I cared about Turgeniev. Such a poseur! Such a hypocrite! It's true he was wonderfully talented, but I keep thinking what a good (cinema play?) *On the Eve* would make.

August 30. We go to Cornwall to-morrow, I suppose. I've re-read my diary. Tell me, Is there a God? I'm old to-night. Ah, I wish I had someone to love me, comfort me and stop me thinking.

[After two changes of rooms in Chelsea, and a fortnight in a furnished cottage at Merryn in Cornwall, we took in September 1914 an ugly cottage at The Lee, near Missenden in Buckinghamshire, where the following entries were written.]

November 3. It's full moon with a vengeance to-night. Out of the front door a field of big turnips, and beyond, a spiky wood with red bands of light behind it. Out of the back door an old tree with just a leaf or two remaining and a moon perched in the branches. I feel very

deeply happy and free. Colette Willy is in my thoughts
to-night. I feel in my own self awake and stretching,
stretching so that I am on tip-toe, full of happy joy.
Can it be that one can renew oneself?

Dear, dear Samuel Butler! Just you wait: I'll do you
proud. To-morrow at about 10.30, I go into action.

November 15. It's very quiet. I've re-read *L'Entrave*.
I suppose Colette is the only woman in France who
does just this. I don't care a fig at present for anyone
I know except her. But the book to be written is still
unwritten. I can't sit down and fire away like J.

November 16. A letter from F. I had not expected it,
and yet, when it came, it seemed quite inevitable—the
writing, the way the letters were made, his confidence,
and his warm sensational life. I wish he were my friend;
he's very near to me. His personality comes right
through his letters to J. and I want to laugh and run
into the road.

December 28. The year is nearly over. Snow has fallen,
and everything is white. It is very cold. I have changed
the position of my desk into a corner. Perhaps I shall
be able to write far more easily here. Yes, this is a good
place for the desk, because I cannot see out of the stupid
window. I am quite private. The lamp stands on one
corner and *in* the corner. Its rays fall on the yellow
and green Indian curtain and on the strip of red

embroidery. The forlorn wind scarcely breathes. I love to close my eyes a moment and think of the land outside, white under the mingled snow and moonlight—the heaps of stones by the roadside white—snow in the furrows. *Mon Dieu!* How quiet and how patient!

JANUARY 1. WHAT A VILE LITTLE DIARY! BUT I am determined to keep it this year. We saw the Old Year out and the New Year in. A lovely night, blue and gold. The church bells were ringing. I went into the garden and opened the gate and nearly—just walked away. J. stood at the window mashing an orange in a cup. The shadow of the rose-tree lay on the grass like a tiny bouquet. The moon and the dew had put a spangle on everything. But just at 12 o'clock I thought I heard footsteps on the road and got frightened and ran back into the house. But nobody passed. J. thought I was a great baby about the whole affair. The ghost of L.M. ran through my heart, her hair flying, very pale, with dark startled eyes.

For this year I have two wishes: to write, to make money. Consider. With money we could go away as we liked, have a room in London, be as free as we liked, and be independent and proud with nobodies. It is only poverty that holds us so tightly. Well, J. doesn't want money and won't earn money. I must. How? First, get this book[1] finished. That is a start. When? At the end of January. If you do that, you are saved. If I wrote night and day I could do it. Yes, I could. Right O!

I feel the new life coming nearer. I believe, just as

---

[1] 'This book' refers, I think, to a novel called 'Maata', of which the two opening chapters and a complete synopsis alone remain.

I always have believed. Yes, it will come. All will be well.

January 2. A horrible morning and afternoon. *Je me sens incapable de tout,* and at the same time I am *just not* writing very well. I must finish my story to-morrow. I ought to work at it all day— yes, all day and into the night if necessary. A vile day. *J'ai envie de prier au bon Dieu comme le vieux père Tolstoi.* Oh, Lord, make me a better creature to-morrow. *Le cœur me monte aux lèvres d'un goût de sang. Je me déteste aujourd'hui.* Dined at L.'s and talked the Island.[1] It is quite real except that some part of me is blind to it. Six months ago I'd have jumped.

The chief thing I feel lately about myself is that I am getting old. I don't feel like a girl any more, or even like a young woman. I feel really quite past my prime. At times the fear of death is dreadful. I feel ever so much older than J. and that he recognizes it, I am sure. He never used to, but now he often talks like a young man to an older woman. Well, perhaps, it's a good thing.

January 3. A cold, ugly day. It was dark soon after two. Spent it trying to write and running from my room

---

[1] A plan, how far serious I cannot say after these years, of making a settlement in some remote island. It was probably of the same order of seriousness as Coleridge's pantisocratic colony on the Susquehannah.

into the kitchen. I could not get really warm. The day felt endless. Read in the evening, and later read with J. a good deal of poetry. If I lived alone I would be very dependent on poetry. Talked over the Island idea with J. For me I know it has come too late.

January 4. Woke early and saw a snowy branch across the window. It is cold, snow has fallen, and now it is thawing. The hedges and the trees are covered with beads of water. Very dark, too, with a wind somewhere. I long to be alone for a bit.

I make a vow to finish a book this month. I'll write all day and at night too, and get it finished. I *swear*.

January 5. Saw the sun rise. A lovely apricot sky with flames in it and then a solemn pink. Heavens, how beautiful! I heard a knocking, and went downstairs. It was Benny cutting away the ivy. Over the path lay the fallen nests—wisps of hay and feathers. He looked like an ivy bush himself. I made early tea and carried it up to J., who lay half awake with crinkled eyes. I feel so full of love to-day after having seen the sun rise.

Evening. Have written a good deal.

January 9. J. went to town. I worked a little—chased the fowls. One brown fowl refused to leave the garden. Long after it *knew* there was no gap in the wire-netting it kept on running up and down. I must not forget that, nor how cold it was, nor how the mud coated my thin shoes. In the evening L. and K. They talked plans; but I felt very antagonistic to the whole affair.

January 10. Windy and dark. . . . At night we went to L.'s. It was a warm night with big drops of rain falling. I didn't mind the going, but the coming back was rather awful. I was unwell, and tired, and my heart could scarcely beat. But we made up a song to keep going. The rain splashed up to my knees, and I was frightened. L. was nice, very nice, sitting with a piece of string in his hand . . .

January 11. I got up in the dark to be ready for my little maid and watch the dawn coming. It wasn't up to much, though. I am wretched. It is a bright, winking day. Oh God, my God, let me work!

Wasted! Wasted!

January 12. Have been in more of a state of virtue to-day. Actually finished the story, *Brave Love*,[1] and I don't know what to make of it even now. Read it to J., who was also puzzled. Violent headache, but rather happy.

January 20. A man outside is breaking stones. The day is utterly quiet. Sometimes a leaf rustles and a strange puff of wind passes the window. The old man chops, chops, as though it were a heart beating out there.

[1] Of this story I have found only the opening pages.

In the afternoon there came a violent storm, but we walked over to C.'s, dined with them and the L.'s and the S.'s and had a play after. Late we went to the L.'s to sleep; very untidy—newspapers and faded mistletoe. I hardly slept at all, but it was nice.

A stormy day. We walked back this morning. It has rained and snowed and hailed and the wind blows. The dog at the mill howls. A man far away is playing the bugle. I have read and sewed to-day, but not written a word. I want to to-night. It is so funny to sit quietly sewing, while my heart is never for a moment still. I am dreadfully tired in head and body. This sad place is killing me. I live upon old made-up dreams; but they do not deceive either of us.

January 21. I am in the sitting-room downstairs. The wind howls outside, but here it is so warm and pleasant. It looks like a real room where real people live. My sewing-basket is on the table: under the bookcase are poked J.'s old house shoes. The black chair, half in shadow, looks as if a happy person had sprawled there. We had roast mutton and onion sauce and baked rice for dinner. It *sounds* right. I have run the ribbons through my underclothes with a hair-pin in the good home way. But my anxious heart is eating up my body, eating up my nerves, eating up my brain. I feel this poison slowly filling my veins—every particle becoming slowly tainted. . . . I am never, never calm, never for an instant. I remember years ago saying I wished I were one of those happy people who can suffer so far and then collapse or become exhausted. But I am just the opposite. The more I suffer, the more of fiery energy I feel to bear it.

January 22. Weather worse than ever. At tea-time I surprised myself by breaking down. I simply felt for a moment overcome with anguish and came upstairs and put my head on the black cushion. My longing for cities engrosses me.

January 23. The old man breaking stones again. A thick white mist reaches the edge of the field.

January 26. Went to London. We found B.C. had arrived; so D. put us up. D.'s flat looks lovely to me. Had tea at the Criterion with C. and D. Had my hands done. In the evening went to the Oxford and saw Marie Lloyd, who was very good. Slept on the big divan in A.'s room. In the afternoon it was very foggy in London; but the relief to be there was immense.

January 27. Met a woman who'd been in the cinema with me—her pink roses in her belt, and hollow lovely eyes and battered hair. I shall not forget her. *No, no.* She was wonderful.[1]

---

[1] She was, probably, the original of Miss Moss in 'Pictures'. In 1913 K.M. had acted as a super in various cinematograph productions.

February 1. A slight attack of 'flu' is bowling me over. There is a glimpse of sun. The trees look as though they were hanging out to dry.

My cold gained on me all day. I read the lonely Nietzsche; but I felt a bit ashamed of my feelings for this man in the past. He is, if you like, 'human, all too human'. Read until late. I felt wretched simply beyond words. Life was like sawdust and sand. Talked short stories to J.

February 2. I feel a bit more cheerful to-day because I don't look quite so revolting as I have done.

No, the day ended in being as bad as ever. For one thing my illness is really severe. I have been embroidering my kimono with black wool. Bah! What rot! What do I care for such rubbish!

February 3. I can do nothing. Have tidied my desk and taken some quinine and that's all. But I know I shall go, because otherwise I'll die of despair. My head is so hot, but my hands are cold. Perhaps I am *dead* and just pretending to live here. There is, at any rate, no sign of life in me.

February 15. Went to London with J.

February 16. Came to Paris.

February 19. Came to Gray.

[An unposted letter written in the diary.]

February 20. England is like a dream. I am sitting at the window of a little square room furnished with a bed, a wax apple, and an immense flowery clock. Outside the window there is a garden full of wall-flowers and blue enamel saucepans. The clocks are striking five and the last rays of sun pour under the swinging blind. It is very hot—the kind of heat that makes one's cheek burn in infancy. But I am so happy I must just send you a word on a spare page of my diary, dear.

I have had some dreadful adventures on my way here because the place is within the Zone of the armies and not allowed to women. The last old Pa-man who saw my passport, 'M. le Colonel', very grand with a black tea-cosy and gold tassel on his head, and smoking what lady novelists call a 'heavy Egyptian cigarette', nearly sent me back.

But, my dear, it's such wonderful country—all rivers and woods and large birds that look blue in the sunlight. I keep thinking of you and L. The French soldiers are *pour rire*. Even when they are wounded they seem to lean out of their sheds and wave their bandages at the train. But I saw some prisoners to-day—not at all funny. Oh, I have so much to tell you I'd better not begin. We shall see each other some day, won't we, darling?

[Another unposted letter.]

I seem to have just escaped the prison cell, J. dearest, —because I find this place is in the zone of the armies and therefore forbidden to women. However, my Aunt's illness pulled me through. I had some really awful moments. Outside the station he was waiting. He merely *sang* (so typical) 'Follow me, but not as though you were doing so' until we came to a tiny toll-house by the river, against which leant a faded cab. But once fed with my suit-case and our two selves, it dashed off like the wind, the door opening and shutting, to his horror, as he is not allowed in cabs. We drove to a village near by, to a large white house where they had taken a room for me—a most extraordinary room furnished with a bed, a wax apple and an immense flowery clock. It's very hot. The sun streams through the blind. The garden outside is full of wall-flowers and blue enamel saucepans. It would make you laugh, too. . . .

[The Journal continues.]

The curious thing is that I could not concentrate on the end of the journey. I simply felt so happy that I leaned out of the window with my arms along the brass rail and my feet crossed and basked in the sunlight and the wonderful country unfolding. At Châteaudun where we had to change I went to the Buffet to drink. A big pale green room with a large stove jutting out and a buffet with coloured bottles. Two women, their arms folded, leaned against the counter. A little boy, very pale, swung from table to table, taking the orders. It was full of soldiers sitting back in their chairs and swinging their legs and eating. The men shouted through the windows.

The little boy favoured me with a glass of horrible black coffee. He served the soldiers with a kind of dreary contempt. In the porch an old man carried a pail of brown spotted fish—large fish, like the fish one sees in glass cases swimming through forests of beautiful pressed seaweed. The soldiers laughed and slapped each other. They tramped about in their heavy boots. The women looked after them, and the old man stood humbly waiting for someone to attend to him, his cap in his hands, as if he knew that the life he represented in his torn jacket, with his basket of fish—his peaceful occupation—did not exist any more and had no right to thrust itself in here.

The last moments of the journey I was very frightened. We arrived at Gray, and one by one, like women going in to see a doctor, we slipped through a door into a hot room completely fitted with two tables and two colonels, like colonels in comic opera, big shiny grey-whiskered men with a touch of burnt-red in their cheeks, both smoking, one a cigarette with a long curly ash hanging from it. He had a ring on his fingers. Sumptuous and omnipotent he looked. I shut my teeth. I kept my fingers from trembling as I handed the passport and the ticket.

'It won't do, it won't do at all,' said my colonel, and looked at me for what seemed an age but in silence. His eyes were like two grey stones. He took my passport to the other colonel, who dismissed the objection, stamped it, and let me go. I nearly knelt on the floor.

By the station he stood, terribly pale. He saluted and smiled and said, 'Turn to the right and follow me as though you were not following.' Then fast we went towards the Suspension Bridge. He had a postman's bag on his back, and a paper parcel. The street was very muddy. From the toll-house by the bridge a scraggy woman, her hands wrapped in a shawl, peered out at us. Against the toll-house leaned a faded cab. 'Montez! vite, vite!' said he. He threw my suit-case, his letter bag and the parcel on to the floor. The driver sprang into activity, lashed the bony horse, and we tore away with both doors flapping and banging. They would not keep shut, and he, who is not supposed to ride in cabs, had to try to hide. Soldiers passed all the time. At the barracks he stopped a moment and a crowd of faces blocked the window. 'Prends ça, mon vieux,' he said, handing over the paper parcel.

Off we flew again. By the river. Down a long strange white street with houses on either side, very fairy in the late sunlight. He said 'I know you will like the house. It's quite white, and so is the room, and the people are, too.'

At last we arrived. The woman of the house, with a serious baby in her arms, came to the door.

'It is all right?'

'Yes, all right. Bonjour, Madame.'

It was like an elopement.

[Katherine Mansfield returned to England at the end of February and left for Paris once more in May.]

Sunday, May 16. *Paris.* I dreamed all night of Rupert Brooke. And to-day as I left the house he was standing at the door, with a rucksack on his back and his hat shading his face. So after I had posted J.'s letter I did not go home. I went a long, very idle sort of amble along the quais. It was exquisitely hot: white clouds lay upon the sky like sheets spread out to dry. On the big sandheaps down by the river children had hollowed out tunnels and caverns. They sat in them, stolid and content, their hair glistening in the sun. Now and then a man lay stretched on his face, his head in his arms. The river was full of big silver stars; the trees shook, faintly glinting with light. I found delightful places— little squares with white square houses. Quite hollow they looked, with the windows gaping open. Narrow streets arched over with chestnut boughs, or perhaps quite deserted, with a clock tower showing over the roofs. The sun put a spell on everything.

I crossed and recrossed the river and leaned over the bridges and kept thinking we were coming to a park when we weren't. You cannot think what a pleasure my invisible, imaginary companion gave me. If he had been alive it would never have possibly occurred; but—it's a game I like to play—to walk and talk with the dead who smile and are silent, and *free*, quite finally free. When I lived alone, I would often come home, put my key in the door, and find someone

47

there waiting for me. 'Hullo! Have you been here long?'

I suppose that sounds dreadful rubbish.

Notre Dame.

I am sitting on a broad bench in the sun hard by Notre Dame. In front of me there is a hedge of ivy. An old man walked along with a basket on his arm, picking off the withered leaves. In the priests' garden they are cutting the grass. I love this big cathedral. The little view I have of it now is of pointed narrow spires, fretted against the blue, and one or two squatting stone parrots balanced on a little balcony. It is like a pen-drawing by a Bogey. And I like the saints with their crowns on their collars and their heads in their hands.

The 'Life' of Life.

I bought a book by Henry James yesterday and read it, as they say, 'until far into the night'. It was not very interesting or very good, but I can wade through pages and pages of dull, turgid James for the sake of that sudden sweet shock, that violent throb of delight that he gives me at times. I don't doubt this is genius: only there is an extraordinary amount of pan and an amazingly *raffiné* flash—

One thing I want to annotate. His hero, Bernard Longueville, brilliant, rich, dark, agile, etc., though a witty companion, is perhaps wittiest and most amused when he is alone, and preserves his best things for himself. . . . All the attributive adjectives apart I am witty, I know, and a good companion—but I feel my case is exactly like his—the amount of minute and delicate joy I get out of watching people and things when I am alone is simply enormous—I really only have 'perfect fun' with myself. When I see a little girl running by on her heels like a fowl in the wet, and say 'My dear, there's a gertie', I laugh and enjoy it as I never would with anybody. Just the same applies to my feeling for what is called 'nature'. Other people won't stop and look at the things I want to look at, or, if they do, they stop to please me or to humour me or to keep the peace. But I am so made that as sure as I am with anyone, I begin to give consideration to their opinions and their desires, and they are not worth half the consideration that mine are. I don't miss J. at all now—I don't want to go home, I feel quite content to live here, in a furnished room, and watch. It's a pure question of weather, that's what I believe. (A *terrific* Gertie has just passed.) Life with other people becomes a blur: it does with J., but it's enormously valuable and marvellous when I'm alone, the detail of life, the *life* of life.

Père de famille.

This family began very modest with Mamma, extremely fat, with a black moustache and a little round toque covered with poached pansies, and the baby boy, bursting out of an English tweed suit that was intended for a Norfolk, but denied its country at the second seam. They had barely settled in their places and pinched every separate piece of bread in the basket and chosen the crustiest when two young men in pale-blue uniforms, with about as much moustache as mother, appeared at the doorway of the restaurant and were hailed with every appearance of enthusiasm by sonny, who waved a serviette about the size of a single bed sheet at them. Mother was embraced; they sat down side by side and were presently joined by an unfortunate overgrown boy whose complexion had enjoyed every possible form of *Frühlingserwachen* and who looked as though he spent his nights under an eiderdown eating chocolate biscuits with the window shut. . . .

Five single bed sheets were tucked into five collars—Five pairs of eyes read over the menu.

Suddenly with a cry of delight up flew Mamma's arms—up flew sonny's—the two young soldiers sprang to their feet, the étudiant came out in no end of a perspiration as a stout florid man appeared, and walked towards them. The waitress hovered round the table, delighted beyond words at this exhibition of vie de famille. She felt like their own bonne—she felt she had known them for years. Heaven knows what memories she had of taking M. Roué his hot water, of being found by M. Paul, looking for his shirt stud on his bedroom floor, on her charming little hands and her still more delicious knees!

THE WAITER

Travelling Alone.

Was it simply her own imagination, or could there
be any truth in this feeling that waiters—waiters
especially and hotel servants—adopted an impertinent,
arrogant and slightly amused attitude towards a woman
who travelled alone? Was it just her wretched female
self-consciousness? No, she really did not think it was.
For even when she was feeling at her happiest, at her
freest, she would become aware, quite suddenly, of the
'tone' of the waiter or the hotel servant. And it was
extraordinary how it wrecked her sense of security, how
it made her feel that something malicious was being
plotted against her and that everybody and everything
—yes, even to inanimate objects like chairs or tables
was merely 'in the know', waiting for that ominous
infallible thing to happen to her, which always did
happen, which was bound to happen, to every woman
on earth who travelled alone!

The waiter prodded a keyhole with a bunch of keys,
wrenched one round, flung the grey-painted door open
and stood against it, waiting for her to pass in. He held
his feather duster upright in his hand like a smoky
torch.

'Here is a nice little room for Madame,' said the
waiter insinuatingly. As she entered, he brushed past
her, opened the groaning window and unhooked the
shutters.

[After some weeks in rooms at Elgin Crescent, in July we took a
house at No. 5 Acacia Road, St. John's Wood. Here Katherine

Mansfield's brother 'Chummie' came to stay with her for a week before going to the front. He was killed almost immediately. The following entry is a record of one of their conversations together.]

Evening.

October. They are walking up and down the garden in Acacia Road. It is dusky; the Michaelmas daisies are bright as feathers. From the old fruit-tree at the bottom of the garden—the slender tree rather like a poplar —there falls a little round pear, hard as a stone.

'Did you hear that, Katie? Can you find it? By Jove —that familiar sound.'

Their hands move over the thin moist grass. He picks it up, and, unconsciously, as of old, polishes it on his handkerchief.

'Do you remember the enormous number of pears there used to be on that old tree?'

'Down by the violet bed.'

'And how after there'd been a Southerly Buster we used to go out with clothes-baskets to pick them up?'

'And how while we stooped they went on falling, bouncing on our backs and heads?'

'And how far they used to be scattered, ever so far, under the violet leaves, down the steps, right down to the lily-lawn? We used to find them trodden in the grass. And how soon the ants got to them. I can see now that little round hole with a sort of fringe of brown pepper round it.'

'Do you know that I've never seen pears like them since?'

'They were so bright, canary yellow—and small. And the peel was so thin and the pips jet—jet black. First you pulled out the little stem and sucked it. It was faintly sour, and then you ate them always from the top—core and all.'

'The pips were delicious.'

'Do you remember sitting on the pink garden seat?'

'I shall never forget that pink garden seat. It is the only garden seat for me. Where is it now? Do you think we shall be allowed to sit on it in Heaven?'

'It always wobbled a bit and there were usually the marks of a snail on it.'

'Sitting on that seat, swinging our legs and eating the pears—'

'But isn't it extraordinary how *deep* our happiness was—how positive—deep, shining, warm. I remember the way we used to look at each other and smile—do you?—sharing a secret . . . What was it?'

'I think it was the family feeling—we were almost like one child. I always see us walking about together, looking at things together with the same eyes, discussing. . . . I felt that again—just now—when we looked for the pear in the grass. I remembered ruffling the violet leaves with you—Oh, that garden! Do you remember that some of the pears we found used to have little teeth-marks in them?'

'Yes.'

'Who bit them?'

'It was always a mystery.'

He puts his arm round her. They pace up and down. And the round moon shines over the pear tree, and the ivy walls of the garden glitter like metal. The air smells chill . . . heavy . . . very cold.

'We shall go back there one day—when it's all over.'

'We'll go back together.'

'And find everything—'

'Everything!'

She leans against his shoulder. The moonlight deepens. Now they are facing the back of the house. A square of light shows in the window.

'Give me your hand. You know I shall always be a stranger here.'

'Yes, darling, I know.'

'Walk up and down once more and then we'll go in.'

'It's so curious—my absolute confidence that I'll come back. I feel it's as certain as this pear.'

'I feel that too.'

'I couldn't not come back. You know that feeling. It's awfully mysterious.'

The shadows on the grass are long and strange; a puff of strange wind whispers in the ivy and the old moon touches them with silver.

She shivers.

'You're cold.'

'Dreadfully cold.'

He puts his arm round her. Suddenly he kisses her—

'Good-bye, darling.'

'Ah, why do you say that?'
'Darling, good-bye . . . good-bye!'

October 29. A misty, misty evening. I want to write down the fact that not only am I not afraid of death—I welcome the idea of death. I believe in immortality because he is not here, and I long to join him. First, my darling, I've got things to do for both of us, and then I will come as quickly as I can. Dearest heart, I know you are there, and I live with you, and I will write for you. Other people are near, but they are not close to me. To you only do I belong, just as *you* belong to me. Nobody knows how often I am with you. Indeed, I am always with you, and I begin to feel that you know— that when I leave this house and this place it will be with you, and I will never even for the shortest space of time be away from you. You have me. You're in my flesh as well as in my soul. I give others my 'surplus' love, but to you I hold and to you I give my deepest love.

[In November Katherine Mansfield gave up the house in Acacia Road, and went to the south of France. I went with her, but returned to England after three weeks.]

November, Bandol, France. Brother. I think I have known for a long time that life was over for me, but I never realized it or acknowledged it until my brother died. Yes, though he is lying in the middle of a little wood in France and I am still walking upright and feeling the sun and the wind from the sea, I am just as much dead as he is. The present and the future mean nothing to me. I am no longer 'curious' about people; I do not wish to go anywhere; and the only possible value that anything can have for me is that it should put me in mind of something that happened or was when he was alive.

'Do you remember, Katie?' I hear his voice in the trees and flowers, in scents and light and shadow. Have people, apart from these far-away people, ever existed for me? Or have they always failed and faded because I denied them reality? Supposing I were to die as I sit at this table, playing with my Indian paper-knife, what would the difference be? No difference at all. Then why don't I commit suicide? Because I feel I have a duty to perform to the lovely time when we were both alive. I want to write about it, and he wanted me to. We talked it over in my little top room in London. I said: I will just put on the front page: To my brother, Leslie Heron Beauchamp. Very well: it shall be done. . . .

The wind died down at sunset. Half a ring of moon hangs in the hollow air. It is very quiet. Somewhere I can hear a woman crooning a song. Perhaps she is crouched before the stove in the corridor, for it is the kind of song that a woman sings before a fire—brooding, warm, sleepy, and safe. I see a little house with flower patches under the windows and the soft mass of a haystack at the back. The fowls have all gone to roost—

they are woolly blurs on the perches. The pony is in the stable with a cloth on. The dog lies in the kennel, his head on his forepaws. The cat sits up beside the woman, her tail tucked in, and the man, still young and careless, comes climbing up the back road. Suddenly a spot of light shows in the window and on the pansy bed below, and he walks quicker, whistling.

But where are these comely people? These young strong people with hard healthy bodies and curling hair? They are not saints or philosophers; they are decent human beings—but where *are they?*

Wednesday. [*December.*] To-day I am hardening my heart. I am walking all round my heart and building up the defences. I do not mean to leave a loophole even for a tuft of violets to grow in. Give me a hard heart, O Lord! Lord, harden thou my heart!

This morning I could walk a little. So I went to the Post Office. It was bright with sun. The palm-trees stood up into the air, crisp and shining; the blue gums hung heavy with sun as is their wont. When I reached the road I heard a singing. A funny thought ... 'The English have come!' But of course, it was not they.

Sunday. [*December.*] Ten minutes past four. I am sure that this Sunday is the worst of all my life. I've touched bottom. Even my heart doesn't beat any longer. I only keep alive by a kind of buzz of blood in my veins. Now the dark is coming back again; only at the windows there is a white glare. My watch ticks loudly and strongly on the bed table, as though it were rich with a minute life, while I faint—I die.

It is evening again. The sea runs very high. It frets, sweeps up and over, hugs, leaps upon the rocks. In the sharp metallic light the rocks have a reddish tinge. Above them a broad band of green mixed with a rich sooty black; above it the cone of a violet mountain; above the mountain a light blue sky shining like the inside of a wet sea-shell. Every moment the light changes. Even as I write, it is no longer hard. Some small white clouds top the mountain like tossed-up smoke. And now a purple colour, very menacing and awful, is pulling over the sky. The trees tumble about in the unsteady light. A dog barks. The gardener, talking to himself, shuffles across the new raked path, picks up his weed basket and goes off. Two lovers are walking together by the side of the sea. They are muffled up in coats. She has a red handkerchief on her head. They walk, very proud and careless, hugging each other and braving the wind.

I am ill to-day—I cannot walk at all—and in pain.

[The illness from which Katherine Mansfield suffered was a rheumatic pain which had a pernicious effect on the action of her heart. It had no connection with the pulmonary tuberculosis of which she died. This did not appear until two years later, in December 1917. Katherine Mansfield was always convinced that she would die of heart failure.]

An Encounter.

This afternoon I did not go for a walk. There is a long stone embankment that goes out into the sea. Huge stones on either side and a little rough goat path in the centre. When I came to the end the sun was going down. So, feeling extremely solitary and romantic, I sat me down on a stone and watched the red sun, which looked horribly like a morsel of tinned apricot, sink into a sea like a huge junket. I began, feebly but certainly perceptibly, to harp: 'Alone between sea and sky etc.' But suddenly I saw a minute speck on the bar coming towards me. It grew, it turned into a young officer in dark blue, slim, with an olive skin, fine eyebrows, long black eyes, a fine silky moustache.

'You are alone, Madame?'

'Alone, Monsieur.'

'You are living at the hotel, Madame?'

'At the hotel, Monsieur.'

'Ah, I have noticed you walking alone several times, Madame.'

'It is possible, Monsieur.'

He blushed and put his hand to his cap.

'I am very indiscreet, Madame.'

'Very indiscreet, Monsieur.'

[At the end of December 1915 I returned to Bandol. There we took a tiny four-roomed villa, Villa Pauline, with an almond-tree that tapped at the window of the *salle à manger*. There we stayed until April 1916; and there K.M. wrote the first version of *Prelude*.]

JANUARY 22. [*VILLA PAULINE, BANDOL.*] NOW, really, what is it that I do want to write? I ask myself. Am I less of a writer than I used to be? Is the need to write less urgent? Does it still seem as natural to me to seek that form of expression? Has speech fulfilled it? Do I ask anything more than to relate, to remember, to assure myself?

There are times when these thoughts half-frighten me and very nearly convince. I say: You are now so fulfilled in your own being, in being alive, in living, in aspiring towards a greater sense of life and a deeper loving, the other thing has gone out of you.

But no, at bottom I am not convinced, for at bottom never has my desire been so ardent. Only the form that I would choose has changed utterly. I feel no longer concerned with the same appearance of things. The people who lived or whom I wished to bring into my stories don't interest me any more. The plots of my stories leave me perfectly cold. Granted that these people exist and all the differences, complexities and resolutions are true to them—why should *I* write about them? They are not near me. All the false threads that bound me to them are cut away quite.

Now—now I want to write recollections of my own country. Yes, I want to write about my own country till I simply exhaust my store. Not only because it is 'a sacred debt' that I pay to my country because my brother and I were born there, but also because in my thoughts I range with him over all the remembered places. I am never far away from them. I long to renew them in writing.

Ah, the people—the people we loved there—of them, too, I want to write. Another 'debt of love'. Oh, I want for one moment to make our undiscovered country leap into the eyes of the Old World. It must be mysterious, as though floating. It must take the breath. It must be 'one of those islands. . . .' I shall tell everything, even of how the laundry-basket squeaked at 75. But all must be told with a sense of mystery, a radiance, an afterglow, because you, my little sun of it, are set. You have dropped over the dazzling brim of the world. Now I must play my part.

Then I want to write poetry. I feel always trembling on the brink of poetry. The almond-tree, the birds, the little wood where you are, the flowers you do not see, the open window out of which I lean and dream that you are against my shoulder, and the times that your photograph 'looks sad'. But especially I want to write a kind of long elegy to you . . . perhaps not in poetry. Nor perhaps in prose. Almost certainly in a kind of *special prose*.

And, lastly, I want to keep a kind of *minute note-book*, to be published some day. That's all. No novels, no problem stories, nothing that is not simple, open.

K.M.

February 13. I have written practically nothing yet, and now again the time is getting short. There is nothing done. I am no nearer my achievement than I was two months ago, and I keep half-doubting my will to perform anything. Each time I make a move my demon says at almost the same moment: 'Oh, yes, we've heard that before!' And then I hear R.B. in the Café Royal, 'Do you still write?' If I went back to England without a book *finished* I should give myself up. I should know that, whatever I said, I was not really a writer and had no claim to 'a table in my room'. But if I go back with a book finished it will be a *profession de foi pour toujours*. Why do I hesitate so long? Is it just idleness? Lack of will-power? Yes, I feel that's what it is, and that's why it's so immensely important that I should assert myself. I have put a table to-day in my room, facing a corner, but from where I sit I can see some top shoots of the almond-tree and the sea sounds loud. There is a vase of beautiful geraniums on the table. Nothing could be nicer than this spot, and it's so quiet and so high, like sitting up in a tree. I feel I shall be able to write here, especially towards twilight.

Ah, once fairly alight—how I'd blaze and burn! Here is a new fact. When I am not writing I feel my brother calling me, and he is not happy. Only when I write or am in a state of writing—a state of 'inspiration'—do I feel that he is calm. . . . Last night I dreamed of him and Father Zossima. Father Zossima said: 'Do not let the new man die.' My brother was certainly there. But last evening he called me while I sat down by the fire. At last I obeyed and came upstairs. I stayed in the dark and waited. The moon got very bright. There were stars outside, very bright twinkling stars, that seemed to move as I watched them. The moon shone. I could see the curve of the sea and the curve of the land embracing, and above in the sky there was a round sweep of cloud. Perhaps those three half-circles were very magic. But then, when I leaned out of the window I seemed to see my brother dotted all over the field— now on his back, now on his face, now huddled up, now half-pressed into the earth. Wherever I looked, there he lay. I felt that God showed him to me like that for some express purpose, and I knelt down by the bed. But I could not pray. I had done no work. I was not in an active state of grace. So I got up finally and went downstairs again. But I was terribly sad. . . . The night before, when I lay in bed, I felt suddenly passionate. I wanted J. to embrace me. But as I turned to speak to him or to kiss him I saw my brother lying fast asleep, and I got cold. That happens nearly always. Perhaps because I went to sleep thinking of him, I woke and was he, for quite a long time. I felt my face was his serious, sleepy face. I felt that the lines of my mouth were changed, and I blinked like he did on waking.

This year I have to make money and get known. I want to make enough money to be able to give L.M.

some. In fact, I want to provide for her. That's my idea, and to make enough so that J. and I shall be able to pay our debts and live honourably. I should like to have a book published and *numbers* of short stories ready. Ah, even as I write, the smoke of a cigarette seems to mount in a reflective way, and I feel nearer that kind of silent, crystallized being that used to be almost me.

February 14. I begin to think of an unfinished memory which has been with me for years. It is a very good story if only I can tell it right, and it is called 'Lena'. It plays in New Zealand and would go in the book. If only I can get right down to it.

Dear brother, as I jot these notes, I am speaking to you. To whom did I always write when I kept those huge complaining diaries? Was it to myself? But now as I write these words and talk of getting down to the New Zealand atmosphere, I see you opposite to me, I see your thoughtful, seeing eyes. Yes, it is to you. We were travelling—sitting opposite to each other and moving very fast. Ah, my darling, how have I kept away from this tremendous joy? Each time I take up my pen *you* are with me. You are mine. You are my playfellow, my brother, and we shall range all over our country together. It is with you that I see, and that is why I see so clearly. That is a great mystery. My brother, I have doubted these last few days. I have been in dreadful places. I have felt that I could not *come* through to you. But now, quite suddenly, the mists are rising, and I see and I know you are near me. You are more vividly with me now this moment than if you were alive and I were writing to you from a short distance away. As you speak my name, the name you call me by that I love so—'Katie!'—your lip lifts in a smile—you believe in me, you know I am here. Oh, Chummie! put your arms round me. I was going to write: Let us shut out everybody. But no, it is not that. Only we shall look on at them together. My brother, you know, with all my desire, my will is weak. To do things—even to write absolutely for myself and by myself—is awfully hard for me. God knows why, when my desire is so strong. But just as it was always our delight to sit together—you remember?—and to talk of the old days, down to the last detail—the last feeling —looking at each other and by our eyes expressing when speech ended how intimately we understood each other —so now, my dear one, we shall do that again. You know how unhappy I have been lately. I almost felt: Perhaps 'the new man' will not live. Perhaps I am not yet risen. . . . But now I do not doubt. It is the idea (it has always been there, but never as it is with me to-night) that I do not write alone. That in every word I write and every place I visit I carry you with me. Indeed, that might be the motto of my book. There are daisies on the table and a red flower, like a poppy, shines through. Of daisies I will write. Of the dark. Of the wind—and the sun and the mists. Of the shadows. Ah!

of all that you loved and that I too love and feel. To-night it is made plain. However often I write and re-write I shall not really falter, dearest, and the book shall be written and ready.

February 15. I have broken the silence. It took long. Did I fail you when I sat reading? Oh, bear with me a little. I will be better. I will do *all*, all that we would wish. Love, I will not fail. To-night it is very wild. Do you hear? It is all wind and sea. You feel that the world is blowing like a feather, springing and rocking in the air like a balloon from Lindsay's. I seem to hear a piano sometimes, but that's fancy. How loud the wind sounds! If I write every day faithfully a little record of how I have kept faith with you—that is what I must do. Now you are back with me. You are stepping forward, one hand in your pocket. My brother, my little boy brother! Your thoughtful eyes! I see you always as you left me. I saw you a moment alone—by yourself—and quite lost, I felt. My heart yearned over you then. Oh, it yearns over you to-night and now! Did you cry? I always felt: He never, never must be unhappy. Now I will come quite close to you, take your hand, and we shall tell this story to each other.

February 16. I *found* 'The Aloe'[1] this morning. And when I had re-read it I knew that I was not quite

---

[1] 'The Aloe' was the original version of *Prelude*. It exists in its original and longer form, and will be published with the remaining fragments of Katherine Mansfield's writings.

'right' yesterday. No, dearest, it was not just the spirit. 'The Aloe' is right. 'The Aloe' is lovely. It simply fascinates me, and I know that it is what you would wish me to write. And now I know what the last chapter is. It is your birth—your coming in the autumn. You in Grandmother's arms under the tree, your solemnity, your wonderful beauty. Your hands, your head—your helplessness, lying on the earth, and, above all, your tremendous solemnity. That chapter will end the book. The next book will be yours and mine. And you must mean the world to Linda; and before ever you are born Kezia must play with you—her little Bogey. Oh, Bogey—I must hurry. All of them must have this book. It is good, my treasure! My little brother, it is good, and it is what we really meant.

February 17. I am sad to-night. Perhaps it is the old forlorn wind. And the thought of you *spiritually* is not enough to-night. I want you by me. I must get deep down into my book, for then I shall be happy. Lose myself, lose myself to find you, dearest. Oh, I want this book to be written. It MUST be done. It must be bound and wrapped and sent to New Zealand. I feel that with all my soul. . . . It will be.

A Recollection of Childhood.

Things happened so simply then, without preparation and without any shock. They let me go into my mother's room (I remember standing on tiptoe and using both hands to turn the big white china door-handle) and there lay my mother in bed with her arms along the sheet, and there sat my grandmother before the fire with a baby in a flannel across her knees. My mother paid no attention to me at all. Perhaps she was asleep, for my grandmother nodded and said in a voice scarcely above a whisper, 'Come and see your little sister.' I tiptoed to her voice across the room, and she parted the flannel, and I saw a little round head with a tuft of goldy hair on it and a big face with eyes shut—white as snow. 'Is it alive?' I asked. 'Of course,' said grandmother. 'Look at her holding my finger.' And—yes, a hand, scarcely bigger than my doll's, in a frilled sleeve, was wound round her finger. 'Do you like her?' said my grandmother. 'Yes. Is she going to play with the doll's house?' 'By and by,' said the grandmother, and I felt very pleased. Mrs. Heywood had just given us the doll's house. It was a beautiful one with a veranda and a balcony and a door that opened and shut and two chimneys. I wanted badly to show it to someone else.

'Her name is Gwen,' said the grandmother. 'Kiss her.'

I bent down and kissed the little goldy tuft. But she took no notice. She lay quite still with her eyes shut.

'Now go and kiss mother,' said the grandmother.

But mother did not want to kiss me. Very languid, leaning against the pillows, she was eating some sago. The sun shone through the windows and winked on the brass knobs of the big bed.

After that grandmother came into the nursery with Gwen, and sat in front of the nursery fire in the rocking-chair with her. Meg and Tadpole were away staying with Aunt Harriet, and they had gone before the new doll's house arrived, so that was why I so longed to have somebody to show it to. I had gone all through it myself, from the kitchen to the dining-room, up into the bedrooms with the doll's lamp on the table, heaps and heaps of times.

'*When* will she play with it?' I asked grandmother.

'By and by, darling.'

It was spring. Our garden was full of big white lilies. I used to run out and sniff them and come in again with my nose all yellow.

'Can't she go out?'

At last, one very fine day, she was wrapped in the warm shawl and grandmother carried her into the cherry orchard, and walked up and down under the falling cherry flowers. Grandmother wore a grey dress with white pansies on it. The doctor's carriage was waiting at the door, and the doctor's little dog, Jackie, rushed at me and snapped at my bare legs. When we went back to the nursery and the shawl was taken away, little white petals like feathers fell out of the folds. But Gwen did not look, even then. She lay in grandmother's arms, her eyes just open to show a line of blue, her face very white, and the one tuft of goldy hair standing up on her head.

All day, all night grandmother's arms were full. I had

no lap to climb into, no pillow to rest against. All belonged to Gwen. But Gwen did not notice this; she never put up her hand to play with the silver brooch that was a half-moon with five little owls sitting on it; she never pulled grandmother's watch from her bodice and opened the back by herself to see grandfather's hair; she never buried her head close to smell the lavender water, or took up grandmother's spectacle case and wondered at its being really silver. She just lay still and let herself be rocked.

Down in the kitchen one day old Mrs. M'Elvie came to the door and asked Bridget about the poor little mite, and Bridget said, 'Kep' alive on bullock's blood hotted in a saucer over a candle'. After that I felt frightened of Gwen, and I decided that even when she did play with the doll's house I would not let her go upstairs into the bedroom—only downstairs, and then only when I saw she could look.

Late one evening I sat by the fire on my little carpet hassock and grandmother rocked, singing the song she used to sing to me, but more gently. Suddenly she stopped and I looked up. Gwen opened her eyes and turned her little round head to the fire and looked and looked at, and then—turned her eyes up to the face bending over her. I saw her tiny body stretch out and her hands flew up, and 'Ah! Ah! Ah!' called the grandmother.

Bridget dressed me next morning. When I went into the nursery I sniffed. A big vase of the white lilies was standing on the table. Grandmother sat in her chair to one side with Gwen in her lap, and a funny little man with his head in a black bag was standing behind a box of china eggs.

'Now!' he said, and I saw my grandmother's face change as she bent over little Gwen.

'Thank you,' said the man, coming out of the bag. The picture was hung over the nursery fire. I thought it looked very nice. The doll's house was in it—veranda and balcony and all. Gran held me up to kiss my little sister.

Recollections of College.

J.'s application is a perpetual reminder to me. Why am I not writing too? Why, feeling so rich, with the greater part of this to be written *before* I go back to England, do I not begin? If only I have the courage to press against the stiff swollen gate all that lies within is mine; why do I linger for a moment? Because I am idle, out of the habit of work and spendthrift beyond belief. Really it is idleness, a kind of immense idleness— hateful and disgraceful.

I was thinking yesterday of my *wasted, wasted* early girlhood. My college life, which is such a vivid and detailed memory in one way, might never have contained a book or a lecture. I lived in the girls, the professor, the big, lovely building,[1] the leaping fires in winter

[1] Queen's College, Harley Street, London.

and the abundant flowers in summer. The views out
of the windows, all the pattern that was—weaving.
Nobody saw it, I felt, as I did. My mind was just like
a squirrel. I gathered and gathered and hid away, for
that long 'winter' when I should rediscover all this
treasure—and if anybody came close I scuttled up the
tallest, darkest tree and hid in the branches. And I was
so awfully fascinated in watching Hall Griffin and all
his tricks—thinking about him as he sat there, his
private life, what he was like as a man, etc., etc. (He
told us he and his brother once wrote an enormous
poem called the Epic of the Hall Griffins.) Then it was
only at rare intervals that something flashed through
all this business, something about Spenser's Faery
Queen or Keats's Isabella and the Pot of Basil, and those
flashes were always when I disagreed flatly with H.G.
and wrote in my notes—This man is a fool. And Cramb,
wonderful Cramb! The figure of Cramb was enough,
he was 'history' to me. Ageless and fiery, eating himself
up again and again, very fierce at what he had seen,
but going a bit blind because he had looked so long.
Cramb striding up and down, filled me up to the brim.
I couldn't write down Cramb's thunder. I simply
wanted to sit and hear him. Every gesture, every
stopping of his walk, all his tones and looks are as vivid
to me as though it were yesterday—but of all he said I
only remember phrases—'He sat there and his wig fell
off—' 'Anne Bullen, a lovely *pure* creature stepping out
of her quiet door into the light and clamour,' and

looking back and seeing the familiar door shut upon her, with a little click as it were—final.

But what coherent account could I give of the history of English Literature? And what of English History? None. When I think in *dates* and *times* the wrong people come in—the right people are missing.[1] When I read a play of Shakespeare I want to be able to place it in relation to what came before and what comes after. I want to realize what England was like then, at least a little, and what the people looked like (but even as I write I feel I can do this, at least the latter thing), but when a man is mentioned, even though the man is real, I don't want to set him on the right hand of Sam Johnson when he ought to be living under Shakespeare's shadow. And this I often do.

Since I came here I have been very interested in the Bible. I have read the Bible for hours on end and I began to do so with just the same desire. I wanted to know if Lot followed close on Noah or something like that. But I feel so bitterly I should have known facts like this: they ought to be part of my breathing. Is there another grown person as ignorant as I? But why didn't I listen to the old Principal who lectured on Bible History twice a week instead of staring at his

---

[1] On the opposite page is a long list of the chief figures in the history of English Literature, working backwards from the eighteenth century. Evidently, Katherine Mansfield had been trying to test her knowledge. In the final result, the list, though it is much corrected, is singularly accurate.

face that was very round, a dark red colour with a kind of bloom on it and covered all over with little red veins with endless tiny tributaries that ran even up his forehead and were lost in his bushy white hair. He had tiny hands, too, puffed up, purplish, shining under the stained flesh. I used to think, looking at his hands—he will have a stroke and die of paralysis. . . . They told us he was a very learned man, but I could not help seeing him in a double-breasted frock-coat, a large pseudo-clerical pith helmet, a large white handkerchief falling over the back of his neck, standing and pointing out with an umbrella a probable site of a probable encampment of some wandering tribe, to his wife, an elderly lady with a threatening heart who had to go everywhere in a basket-chair arranged on the back of a donkey, and his two daughters, in thread gloves and sand shoes—smelling faintly of some anti-mosquito mixture.

As he lectured I used to sit, building his house, peopling it—filling it with Americans, ebony and heavy furniture—cupboards like tiny domes and tables with elephants' legs presented to him by grateful missionary friends. . . . I never came into contact with him but once, when he asked any young lady in the room to hold up her hand if she had been chased by a wild bull, and as nobody else did I held up mine (though of course I hadn't). 'Ah,' he said, 'I am afraid you do not count. You are a little savage from New Zealand'—which was a trifle exacting, for it must be the rarest thing to be chased by a wild bull up and down Harley Street,

Wimpole Street, Welbeck Street, Queen Anne, round and round Cavendish Square. . . .

And why didn't I learn French with M. Huguenot? What an opportunity missed! What has it not cost me! He lectured in a big narrow room that was painted all over—the walls, door, and window-frames, a grey shade of mignonette green. The ceiling was white, and just below it there was a frieze of long looped chains of white flowers. On either side of the marble mantelpiece a naked small boy staggered under a big platter of grapes that he held above his head. Below the windows, far below there was a stable court paved in cobble-stones, and one could hear the faint clatter of carriages coming out or in, the noise of water gushing out of a pump into a big pail—some youth, clumping about and whistling. The room was never very light, and in sum-mer M.H. liked the blinds to be drawn half-way down the window. . . . He was a little fat man.

The old man could not get over the fact that he was still strong enough to lift such a lump of a boy. He wanted to do it again and again, and even when the little boy was awfully tired of the game the old man kept putting out his arms and smiling foolishly and trying to lift him still higher. He even tried with one arm. . . .

Saunders Lane.
March 12. Our house in Tinakori Road stood far back from the road. It was a big, white-painted square house

with a slender pillared veranda and balcony running all the way round it. In the front from the veranda edge the garden sloped away in terraces and flights of concrete steps—down—until you reached the stone wall covered with nasturtiums that had three gates let into it—the visitors' gate, the Tradesman's gate, and a huge pair of old iron gates that were never used and clashed and clamoured when Bogey and I tried to swing on them.

Tinakori Road was not fashionable; it was very mixed. Of course there were some good houses in it, old ones, like ours for instance, hidden away in wildish gardens, and there was no doubt that land there would become extremely valuable, as Father said, if one bought enough and hung on.

It was high, it was healthy; the sun poured in all the windows all day long, and once we had a decent tramway service, as Father argued . . .

But it was a little trying to have one's own washer-woman living next door who would persist in attempting to talk to Mother over the fence, and then, just beyond her 'hovel', as Mother called it, there lived an old man who burned leather in his back yard whenever the wind blew our way. And further along there lived an endless family of half-castes who appeared to have planted their garden with empty jam tins and old saucepans and black iron kettles without lids. And then just opposite our house there was a paling fence, and below the paling fence in a hollow, squeezed in almost under the fold of a huge gorse-covered hill, was Saunders Lane.

[K.M. seems to have made this the scene of her story, *The Garden Party*.]

March. Jinnie Moore was awfully good at elocution. Was she better than I? I could make the girls cry when I read Dickens in the sewing class, and she couldn't. But then she never tried to. She didn't care for Dickens; she liked something about horses and tramps and ship-wrecks and prairie fires—they were her style, her reckless, red-haired, dashing style.

[The following is an unposted letter written to Frederick Goodyear, a close friend of both Katherine Mansfield and myself. He was at this time serving in France in the meteorological section of the Royal Engineers. A few months afterwards he applied for a commission in an infantry regiment in order to go to the fighting line. There he was killed, in May 1917. It should be put on record that no single one of Katherine Mansfield's friends who went to the war returned alive from it. This will explain the profound and ineradicable impression made upon her by the war, an impression which found utterance in the last year of her life in the story, 'The Fly'.

Frederick Goodyear, who was three years my senior at Brasenose, was certainly the most brilliant undergraduate at Oxford in my time. He was the first of my friends to be introduced to Katherine Mansfield after I had made her acquaintance, and he became her friend. He accompanied us to Paris on our unfortunate expedition in the winter of 1913. His letters and literary remains, with a biographical memoir by Mr. F. W. Leith-Ross, were published in 1920. The concluding words of his letter to Katherine Mansfield, to which hers was a reply, are these:

'The fact is I'm simply in a chronic surly temper with life: and NOTHING, if I can possibly help it, shall make me emerge.

'We want a definition. If love is only love when it is resistless, I don't love you. But if it is a relative emotion, I do.

'Personally, I think everything everywhere is bunkum.

'FREDK. GOODYEAR.']

Sunday. Villa Pauline, Bandol (Var). Mr. F.G., Never did cowcumber lie more heavy on a female's buzzum than your curdling effugion which I have read twice and won't again if horses drag me. But I keep wondering, and can't for the life of me think, whatever there was in mine to so importantly disturb you. (Henry James is dead. Did you know?) I did not, swayed by a resistless passion, say that I loved you. Nevertheless I am prepared to say it again looking at this pound of onions that hangs in a string kit from a saucepan nail. But why should you write to me as though I'd got into the family way and driven round to you in a hansom cab to ask you to make a respectable woman of me? Yes, you're bad tempered, suspicious, and surly. And if you think I flung my bonnet over you as a possible mill, my lad, you're mistook.

In fact, now I come to ponder on your last letter I don't believe you want to write to me at all, and I'm hanged if I'll shoot arrows in the air. But perhaps that is temper on my part; it is certainly pure stomach. I'm so hungry, simply empty, and seeing in my mind's eye just now a sirloin of beef, well browned with plenty of gravy *and* horseradish sauce and baked potatoes, I nearly sobbed. There's nothing here to eat except omelettes and oranges and onions. It's a cold, sunny, windy day—the kind of day when you want a tremendous feed for lunch and an arm-chair in front of the fire to boa-constrict in afterwards. I feel sentimental about England now—English food, *decent* English *waste!* How much better than these thrifty French, whose flower gardens are nothing but potential salad bowls. There's not a leaf in France that you can't 'faire une infusion avec', not a blade that isn't 'bon pour la cuisine'. By God, I'd like to buy a pound of the best butter, put it on the window sill and watch it melt to spite 'em. They are a stingy uncomfortable crew for all their lively scrapings. . . . For instance, their houses—what appalling furniture—and never one comfortable chair. If you want to talk the only possible thing to do is to go to bed. It's a case of either standing on your feet or lying in comfort under a puffed-up eiderdown. I quite understand the reason for what is called French moral laxity. You're simply forced into bed—no matter with whom. There's no other place for you. Supposing a *young* man comes to see about the electric light and will go on talking and pointing to the ceiling—or a friend drops in to tea and asks you if you believe in Absolute Evil. How can you give your mind to these things when you're sitting on four knobs and a square inch of cane? How much better to lie snug and *give yourself up to it.*

Later.

Now I've eaten one of the omelettes and one of the oranges. The sun has gone in; it's beginning to thunder.

There's a little bird on a tree outside this window not so much singing as sharpening a note. He's getting a very fine point on it; I expect you would know his name. . . . Write to me again when everything is not *too* bunkum.

Good-bye for now!

With my strictly relative love

K. M.

Notes on Dostoevsky.

March. Nastasya Filipovna Barashkov ('The Idiot').

Page 7. She is first mentioned by Rogozhin in the train, and she is immediately 'recognized' by a man with a red nose and a pimpled face who 'knows all about her'.

'Armance and Coralie and Princess Patsy *and* Nastasya Filipovna.'

'We'll go and see Nastasya Filipovna.' *Prophetic words*.

Page 9. Why did she accept the ear-rings from a man she had never seen? She was not greedy for jewels. She had plenty, and she was extremely particular in her conduct towards other men. Is that a kind of Russian custom? To accept the ear-rings as a kind of recognition of her beauty?

Pages 26, 27. The Portrait: 'Dark and deep, passionate and disdainful.'

Page 33. 'Her face is cheerful, but she has passed through terrible suffering, hasn't she? . . . It's a proud face, awfully proud, but I don't know whether she is good-hearted. Ah! If she were! That would redeem it all.'

Page 37. The Story of Nastasya. That change in her when she appears in Petersburg—her knowledge, almost 'technical', of how things are done in the world, is not at all impossible. With such women it seems to be a kind of instinct. (Maata was just the same. She simply knew these things from nowhere.) Her action, that Dostoevsky says is 'from spite', is to shew her power, and that when he has jerked out the weapon with which he wounded her she feels the dreadful smart.

Having read the whole of 'The Idiot' through again, and fairly carefully, I feel slightly more bewildered than I did before as regards Nastasya Filipovna's character. She is really not well done. She is badly done. And there grows up as one reads on a kind of irritation, a *balked* fascination, which almost succeeds finally in blotting out those first and really marvellous 'impressions' of her. What was Dostoevsky really aiming at?

Shatov and his Wife ('The Possessed').

There is something awfully significant about the attitude of Shatov to his wife, and it is amazing how, when Dostoevsky at last turns a soft but penetrating and full light upon him, how we have managed to gather a great deal of knowledge of his character from the former vague side-lights and shadowy impressions. He is just what we thought him; he behaves just as we would expect him to do. There is all that crudity and what you might call 'shock-headedness' in his nature—and it is wonderfully tragic that he who is so soon to be destroyed himself should suddenly realize— and through a third person—through a little squealing baby—the miracle just being alive is.

Every time I read those chapters about his new-born happiness I cherish a kind of tiny hope that this time he will escape—he will be warned, he won't die.

How did Dostoevsky know about that extraordinary vindictive feeling, that relish for little laughter—that comes over women in pain? It is a very secret thing, but it's profound, profound. They don't want to spare the one whom they love. If that one loves them with a kind of blind devotion as Shatov did Marie, they long to torment him, and this tormenting gives them real positive relief. Does this resemble in any way the tormenting that one observes so often in his affairs of passion? Are his women ever happy when they torment their lovers? No, they too are in the agony of labour. They are giving birth to their new selves. And they never believe in their deliverance.

[After our return from Bandol in April 1916, we lived at Higher Tregerthen in North Cornwall, then at Mylor in South Cornwall. In September 1916 we came to London.]

[*November. 3 Gower Street.*] It is so strange! I am suddenly back again, coming into my room and desiring to write, *Knock*, goes Miss Chapman at the door. A man has come to clean the windows. I might have known it!

And so death claims us. I am sure that just at that final moment a knock will come and Somebody Else will come to 'clean the windows'.

B. has given me his fountain-pen. The room is full of smoke to-night, the gas bubbles as if the pipes were full of water. It's very quiet. I have rather a cold, but I feel absolutely alive after my experience of this afternoon.

December 8. I thought and thought this morning but to not much avail. I can't think why, but my wit seems to be nearly deserting me when I want to get down to earth. I am all right—sky-high. And even in my brain, in my head, I can think and act and write wonders— wonders; but the moment I really try to put them down I fail miserably.

[In the spring of 1917 Katherine Mansfield took a studio for herself in Church Street, Chelsea, while I had rooms near by in Redcliffe Road.]

Summer.

> 'Et pourtant, il faut s'habituer à vivre,
> Même seul, même triste, indifférent et las,
> Car, ô ma vision troublante, n'es-tu pas
> Un mirage incessant trop difficile à suivre?'

[The stories referred to in the following note were, so far as I know, never finished. All that remains of them is a page of MS. from 'Geneva'. I do not understand the whole of the note, which is written in the compressed and cryptic manner Katherine Mansfield sometimes used in sketching out stories. The little boy's remark about the teapot and the kitten appears in 'Mr. Reginald Peacock's Day', *Bliss*, p. 205.]

TCHEHOV MAKES ME FEEL THAT THIS LONGING to write stories of such uneven length is quite justified. *Geneva* is a long story, and *Hamilton* is very short, and this ought to be written to my brother really, and another about the life in New Zealand. Then there is Bavaria. 'Ich liebe Dich, Ich liebe Dich,' floating out on the air . . . and then there is Paris. God! When shall I write all these things and how?

Is that all? Can that be all? That is not what I meant at all.

Tchehov is quite right about women; yes, he is quite right. These fairies in black and silver—'and then, tearing down the road, her long brown fur blowing behind her, brushing the leaves with her trailing skirt, crying: of course he was awfully sorry that she did not get satisfaction, just as he would have been awfully sorry if she hadn't liked strawberries and cream—Friday —Friday—he could not get the word out of his head . . . and before him stood the little man with his hair neatly combed, saying: "Please take something to eat!"' But I cannot believe that at this stage of the proceedings something pretty extraordinary did not happen. I sat with my back to no one.

T.F.; M.F. This woman I know very well—vain, eager, beautiful, *désenchantée*, an 'actress'.

'I can put a little child's bed into the corner.'

'Which do you like best, Daddie—cats or dogs?'

'Well, I think I like dogs best, old chap.'

'I don't: I'd like to have a kitten about as big as a little tea-pot.'

One character, of the man, rather beats me. I want a very quiet man, absorbed in his work, who, once he realized—really realized—that his wife had married him for her own ends, had no more to do with her, but still loved her and adored the child. It is all a bit difficult to write, but awfully fascinating, and should not be at too great length.

Does this pen write? Oh, I do hope so. For it's really beastly to have a pen that doesn't. And then a clergyman goes up to him and says he has lost the tails off his sheep. Well, it's a comic! You see?

August 21. 141 A *Church St., Chelsea.* I came home this afternoon and F. came in. I was standing in the studio, someone whistled on the path. It was he. I went out and bought some milk and honey and Veda bread. By and by we sat down and had tea and talk. This man is in many ways extraordinarily like me. I like him so much; I feel so *honest* with him that it's simply one of my real joys, one of the real joys of my life, to have him come and talk and be with me. I did not realize, until he was here and we ate together, how much I cared for him—and how much I was really at home with him. A real understanding. We might have spoken a different language—returned from a far country. I just felt all was well, and we understood each other. Just that. And there was 'ease' between us. There is a division: people who are my people, people who are not my people. He is mine. I gave him for a pledge my little puddock.[1]

When we walked out I saw the sky again after all the day's blindness—little clouds and big clouds. We said good-bye at Vinden's. That is all. But I wanted to make a note of it.

    I. They meet and just touch.

    II. They come together and part.

    III. They are separated and meet again.

    IV. They realize their tie.

[1] A brass frog which was one of Katherine Mansfield's treasured possessions.

Alors, je pars.

It is astonishing how violently a big branch shakes when a silly little bird has left it. I expect the bird knows it and feels immensely arrogant. The way he went on, my dear, when I said I was going to leave him. He was quite desperate. But now the branch is quiet again. Not a bud has fallen, not a twig has snapped. It stands up in the bright air, steady and firm, and thanks the Lord that it has got its evenings to itself again.

A Shilling gone Bust.

A knock at the door. Two sisters of Nazareth—one, rather pretty and meek, in the background, attending; the other very voluble and fluent, her hands in her sleeves. When she smiled, showing her pale gums and big discoloured teeth I decided that I had quite got over my sentimental feeling about nuns. She was collecting for their home for little children. All sorts of little children were admitted except those suffering from infectious diseases or subject to fits. I wondered what would happen if one developed fits after admittance and decided that I should have the most realistic fit the moment the Nazarene door shut on me. . . . I remember you well from last year, said the nun. But I wasn't here last year. Ah, people change so quickly, said she. Yes, but perhaps their faces don't, said I, seriously, giving her the shilling I was just going to put into the gas meter. I wish I had put it into the gas meter five minutes before. . . .

Living Alone.

Even if I should, by some awful chance, find a hair upon my bread and honey—at any rate it is my own hair.

Beware of the Rain!

Late in the evening, after you have cleared away your supper, blown the crumbs out of the book that you were reading, lighted the lamp and curled up in front of the fire, that is the moment to beware of the rain.

E. M. Forster.

Putting my weakest books to the wall last night I came across a copy of 'Howard's End' and had a look into it. But it's not good enough. E. M. Forster never gets any further than warming the teapot. He's a rare fine hand at that. Feel this teapot. Is it not beautifully warm? Yes, but there ain't going to be no tea.

Love and Mushrooms.

If only one could tell true love from false love as one can tell mushrooms from toadstools. With mushrooms it is so simple—you salt them well, put them aside and have patience. But with love, you have no sooner lighted on anything that bears even the remotest resemblance to it than you are perfectly certain it is not only a genuine specimen, but perhaps *the* only genuine mushroom ungathered. It takes a dreadful number of toadstools to make you realize that life is not one long mushroom.

Babies and the dear old Queen.

Whenever I see babies in arms I am struck again by their resemblance to the dear old Queen. They have just the same air of false resignation, the same mournful, regal plumpness. If only her Majesty had deigned to be photographed in a white woollen bonnet with a little frill of eiderdown round it there'd be no telling the difference. Especially if she could have been persuaded to sit on Grandpa Gladstone's knee for the occasion.

Dreams and Rhubarb.

My sticks of rhubarb were wrapped up in a copy of the *Star* containing Lloyd George's last, *more* than eloquent speech. As I snipped up the rhubarb my eye fell, was fixed and fastened, on that sentence wherein he tells us that we have grasped our niblick and struck out for the open course. Pray Heaven there is some faithful soul ever present with a basket to catch these tender blossoms as they fall. Ah, God! it is a dreadful thought that these immortal words should go down into the dreamless dust uncherished. I loved to think, as I put the rhubarb into the saucepan, that years hence—P.G. many many years hence—when in the fullness of time, full of ripeness and wisdom, the Almighty sees fit to gather him into His bosom, some gentle stone-cutter living his quiet life in the little village that had known great David as a child would take a piece of fair white marble and engrave upon it two niblicks crossed and underneath:

In the hour of England's most imminent peril he grasped his Niblick and struck out for the Open Course.

But what does rather worry me, I thought, turning the gas down to a pinch as the rhubarb began to boil, is how these mighty words are to be translated so that our allies may taste the full flavour of them. Those crowds of patient Russians, waiting in the snow, perhaps, to have the speech read aloud to them—what dreadful weapon will it present to their imagination? Unless *The Daily News* suggests to Mr. Ransome that he walk down the Nevsky Prospekt with a niblick instead of an umbrella for all the world to see. And the French—what *espèce de Niblickisme* will they make of it. Shall we read in the French papers next week of someone *qui manque de niblick*. Or that *'Au milieu de ces événements si graves ce qu'il nous faut c'est du courage, de l'espoir et du niblick le plus ferme. . . .'* I wondered, taking off the rhubarb.

A Victorian Idyll.

> Yesterday Matilda Mason
> In the Parlour by herself
> Broke a Handsome China Basin
> Placed upon the Mantelshelf.

You picture Matilda in a little check dress, puce shoulder ties, muslin pantalettes, black sandals, and a pound of rich glossy curls held in place by a velvet band. She tiptoes about the parlour, among the what-nots and antimacassars and embroidery frames and Mamma's work-box with the ivory fittings, and Papa's music stand with the pearl-studded flute lying across it. . . . How did she come to be in the parlour by herself? Rash, foolish child! Why was she not sitting upon a bead hassock in the nursery conning over one of those amiable little tunes for infants from one and a half to three years (Charles: Pray, dear papa! what is the Solar System? Papa: Wipe your nose, Charles, and I will tell you) or embroidering God is Love in red upon a night-dress case for her dear Mamma?

She had parted her Papa's Piccadilly weepers, had been strained to his flashing bosom before he dashed off to that mysterious place, the City, where ladies feared to tread; her Mamma, having seen the doctor's gig draw up at number twelve, had put on her second best pair of jet ear-rings, wrapped herself in her second best cashmere shawl and taken a flask of eau-de-cologne. . . .

[In November 1917 K.M. caught a chill, which developed into pleurisy. When she had partly recovered the doctor advised her to go to the South of France.

She was overjoyed at the prospect. She did not realize, neither did anybody warn her, that during the two years since she was last in Bandol conditions in France had utterly changed. Railway travelling was difficult, food bad. And, perhaps most serious of all, she would not admit that she was gravely ill. Her courage and confidence deceived herself as well as her friends. She persuaded herself and them that she was the one to be envied for being sent into the sun.

After an appalling journey, described in one of her letters, she reached Bandol in January 1918 to find that the little Mediterranean town she remembered so beautiful was now dirty and neglected. From the moment she arrived she was seriously ill and quite alone, until in February her friend, L.M., managed to get to her.]

[*JANUARY. BANDOL.*] WHEN I AM SITTING ABOVE the rocks near the edge of the sea, I always fancy that I hear above the plash of the water the voice of two people talking somewhere I know not what. And the talking is always broken by something which is neither laughter nor sobbing, but a low thrilling sound which might be either and is a part of both.

But Lord! Lord! how I do hate the French.

Mademoiselle complains that she has the *pieds glacés*.

'Then why do you wear such pretty stockings and shoes, Mademoiselle?' leers Monsieur.

'Eh—o, la—c'est la mode!'

And the fool grins, well content with the idiot answer.

How immensely easier it is to attack an insect that is running away from you rather than one that is running towards you.

Note: A muff like a hard nut. (Mouse in *Je ne parle pas*.)

(*February*.) What happens is that I come in absolutely exhausted, lie down, sit up and sit in a daze of fatigue—a horrible state—until 7 o'clock. I can barely walk—can't think, don't dare to go to sleep because if I do I know I'll lie awake through the night, and that is my horror. Oh, for a *sofa* or a very comfortable arm-chair—this is always the longing at the back of my mind; and except for that and a feeling of despair at wasting the time I am simply a blank. The pain continues in my left shoulder and is *the* . . . That adds, of course, for finally it becomes intolerable and drives me to lie on the bed covered over to support it. But these are, *Hard Lines*.

Verses Writ in a Foreign Bed.

Almighty Father of All and Most Celestial Giver
  Who has granted to us thy children a heart and lungs and a liver;
If upon me should descend thy beautiful gift of tongues
  Incline not thine Omnipotent ear to my remarks on lungs.

'Toujours fatiguée, Madame?'
'Oui, toujours fatiguée.'
'Je ne me lève pas, Victorine; et le courrier?'
Victorine smiles meaningly, 'Pas encore passé.'

February 19. I woke up early this morning and when I opened the shutters the full round sun was just risen. I began to repeat that verse of Shakespeare's: 'Lo, here the gentle lark weary of rest', and bounded back into bed. The bound made me cough—I spat—it tasted strange—it was bright red blood. Since then I've gone on spitting each time I cough a little more. Oh, yes, of course I am frightened. But for two reasons only. I don't want to be ill, I mean 'seriously', away from J. J. is the first thought. 2nd, I don't want to find this is real consumption, perhaps it's going to gallop—who knows? —and I shan't have my work written. *That's what matters.* How unbearable it would be to die—leave 'scraps', 'bits' . . . nothing real finished.

But I feel the first thing to do is to get back to J. Yes, my right lung hurts me badly, but it always does more or less. But *J. and my work*—they are all I think of (mixed with curious visionary longings for gardens in full flower). L.M. has gone for the doctor.

I *knew* this would happen. Now I'll say why. On my way here, in the train from Paris to Marseilles I sat in a carriage with two women. They were both dressed in black. One was big, one little. The little spry one had a sweet smile and light eyes. She was extremely pale, had been ill—was come to repose herself. The Big One, as the night wore on, wrapped herself up in a black shawl—so did her friend. They shaded the lamp and started (trust 'em) talking about illnesses. I sat in the corner feeling damned ill myself.

Then the big one, rolling about in the shaking train, said what a *fatal place* this coast is for anyone who is even threatened with lung trouble. She reeled off the most hideous examples, especially one which froze me finally, of an American *belle et forte avec une simple bronchite* who came down here to be cured and in three weeks had had a severe hæmorrhage and *died*. 'Adieu mon mari, adieu mes beaux enfants.'

This recital, in that dark moving train, told by that big woman swathed in black, had an effect on me that I wouldn't own and never mentioned. I knew the woman was a fool, hysterical, morbid, *but I believed her;* and her voice has gone on somewhere echoing in me ever since. . . .

Juliette has come in and opened the windows; the sea is so full of 'little laughs' and in the window space some tiny flies are busy with their darting, intricate dance.

[Juliette was the little maid at the hotel who devoted herself to Katherine Mansfield. There are many charming pictures of her in the letters of this time.

At last, after many wearing delays, Katherine Mansfield received permission from the 'authorities' to return to England. On the day, however, on which she reached Paris, the long-range bombardment of the city began, and all civilian traffic between Paris and London was instantly suspended. For nearly three weeks she was detained in Paris, exhausted by her illness, yet continually having to visit various 'authorities' for permission either to stay or to depart. She managed to get to London on April 11, a shadow of herself. The ravages of four months' anxiety and illness had been terrible.]

April 2. Paris. I am not doing what I swore I would at

Bandol. I must again write the word

DISCIPLINE

and under that

WHICH DO YOU PREFER?

And from day to day after this keep a strict account of what it is that I fail in. I have failed very badly these last few days and this evening was a 'comble'. *This* to the uninitiated would appear great rubbish. They'd suspect me of God knows what. If only they knew the childish truth! But they won't know. Now, Katherine, here goes for to-morrow—Keep it up, my girl. It's such a chance, now that L.M. is not I-spy-I.

April 3rd. A good day.

He woke, but did not move. Warm and solemn he lay, with wide open troubled eyes, pouting a little, almost frowning for one long moment. In that long moment he sprang out of bed, bathed, dressed, reached the wharf, boarded the ferry boat, crossed the harbour and was waving—waving to Isabel and Maisie who stood there, waiting for him on the pier. A tall young sailor, standing near him, threw a coil of tarred rope and it fell in a long loop, over a landing post. . . . Beautifully done. . . . And all this moment (vision) was so clear and bright and tiny, he might with his flesh and pout and solemn eyes have been a baby watching a bubble.

'I'm there—I'm there. Why do I have to start and do it all so slowly all over again?' But as he thought he moved and the bubble vanished and was forgotten. He sat up in bed smiling, pulling down his pyjama sleeves.

'Je me repose.'

April 25. 'Well sit down, Mansfield, and *reposez-vous*,' said F., 'and I'll get on with my dressing.'

So he went into his bedroom and shut the door between, and I sat on the end of the sofa. The sun came full through the two windows, dividing the studio into four—two quarters of light and two of shadow, but all those things which the light touched seemed to float in it, to bathe and to sparkle in it as if they belonged not to land, but to water; they even seemed, in some strange way, to be moving.

When you lean over the edge of the rock and see something lovely and brilliant flashing at the bottom of the sea it is only the clear, trembling water that dances —but—can you be quite sure? ... No, not quite sure, and that little Chinese group on the writing-table may or may not have shaken itself awake for just one hundredth of a second out of hundreds of years of sleep.

Very beautiful, O God! is a blue tea-pot with two white cups attending; a red apple among oranges addeth fire to flame—in the white bookcases the books fly up and down in scales of colour, with pink and lilac notes recurring, until nothing remains but them, sounding over and over.

There are a number of frames, some painted and some plain, leaning against the wall, and the picture of a naked woman with her arms raised, languid, as though her heavy flowering beauty were almost too great to bear. There are two sticks and an umbrella in one corner, and in the fireplace, a kettle, curiously like a bird.

White net curtains hang over the windows. For all the sun it is raining outside. The gas in the middle of the room has a pale yellow paper shade, and as F. dresses he keeps up a constant whistling.

Reposez-vous.

Oui, je me repose. . . .

April 26. If I had my way I should stay in the Redcliffe Road until after the war. It suits me. Whatever faults it has it is not at all bourgeois. There is 'something a bit queer' about all the people who live in it; they are all more or less 'touched'. They walk about without their hats on and fetch and carry their food and even their coal. There are nearly four bells to every door—the curtains are all 'odd' and shabby. The charwomen, blown old flies, buzz down each other's basements. . . . 'No. 56 'ad a party last night. You never seen anything like the stite of 'is room this morning. . . .' '. . . 'Igh time 'e did get married, I say. 'Is fiangse spends the night with 'im already. 'E says she 'as 'is bed and 'e sleeps on the table. You don't tell me a great stick of a fellow like 'im sleeps on 'is table!'

Question: But do you like this sort of talk? This kind of thing? What about the Poets and—flowers and trees?

Answer: As I can't have the perfect other thing, I *do* like this. I feel, somehow, free in it. It has no abiding place, and neither have I. And—and—Oh well, I *do* feel so cynical.

[Since it was out of the question that K.M. should remain in my two dark ground-floor rooms in Redcliffe Road, she went on May 17 to Looe in Cornwall, while I searched for a house in Hampstead.]

May 21. [*Looe, Cornwall.*] . . . I positively feel, in my hideous modern way, that I can't get into touch with my mind. I am standing gasping in one of those disgusting telephone boxes and I can't 'get through'.

'Sorry. There's no reply,' tinkles out the little voice.

'Will you ring them again—Exchange? A good long ring. There must be somebody there.'

'I can't get any answer.'

Then I suppose there is nobody in the building—nobody at all. Not even an old fool of a watchman. No, it's dark and empty and quiet . . . above all—empty.

Note: A queer thing is that I keep seeing it—this empty building—as my father's office. I smell it as that. I see the cage of the clumsy wooden goods lift and the tarred ropes hanging.

May 22. The sea here is real sea. It rises and falls with a loud noise, has a long, silky roll on it as though it purred, seems sometimes to climb half up into the sky and you see the sail boats perched upon clouds—like flying cherubs.

Hallo! here come two lovers. She has a pinched-in waist, a hat like a saucer turned upside-down—he sham panama, hat-guard, cane, etc.; his arm enfolding. Walking between sea and sky. His voice floats up to me: 'Of course, occasional tinned meat does not matter, but a perpetual diet of tinned meat is bound to produce . . .'

I am sure that the Lord loves them and that they and their seed will prosper and multiply for ever and ever. . . .

[Those of the following phrases which are marked K.M. (by herself) are her own. One or two of the rest may be quotations.]

. . . to meet, on the stopping of the chariot, the august emergence.

The jewel wrapped up in a piece of old silk and negotiable one day in the market of misery.

Luxuriant complications which make the air too tropical. . . .

The sense of folded flowers . . . as though the night had laid its hand upon their hearts and they were folded and at peace like folded flowers. (K.M.)

. . . plucked her sensations by the way, detached, nervously, the small wild blossoms of her dim forest.

The high luxury of not having to explain. . . .

The ostrich burying its head in the sand does at any rate wish to convey the impression that its head is the most important part of it. (K.M. Good.)

Though she did in a way, simply offer herself to me she was so cold, so rich, so splendid, that I simply couldn't see a spoon silver enough to dare help myself with. . . . (K.M.)

If there were going to be large freedoms she was determined to enjoy them too. She wasn't going to be perched, swaying perilous in the changing jungle like a little monkey dropped from a tree on to an elephant's head—and positively clinging to some large ear. (K.M.)

She was the same through and through. You could go on cutting slice after slice and you knew you would never light upon a plum or a cherry or even a piece of peel.

Our friends are only a more or less imperfect embodiment of our ideas. . . .

June. Looe. Feature Extraordinary: Shoes that have never squeaked before start up a squeaking.

A cold day—the cuckoo singing and the sea like liquid metal. Everything feels detached—uprooted—flying through the hurtling air or about to fly. There's almost a sense of having to dodge these unnatural rudderless birds. . . . To use a homely image, imagine the world an immense drying ground with everything blown off the lines. . . . It is very nervously exhausting.

And the day spent itself. . . . The idle hours blew on it and it shed itself like seed. . . .

[Mrs. Honey, in the following note, was the chambermaid in the hotel at Looe, and like most of her servants, devoted to Katherine Mansfield.]

Later.

Mrs. Honey explains. She has been crying. Madame spoke to her 'awful crool' about a cracked tumbler. Lied. Bullied. And the poor old creature, who has had 15 rooms to do lately and three flights of stairs to scrub (age 68) 'couldn't help but cry. . . .'

I wish Madame would develop a tumour during the night, have it cut out to-morrow and be 'dead, buried and a',' before the Sunday dinner. She is exactly like a large cow in a black silk dress—and she will *never*, NEVER, NEVER die.

'If the fire turns bright, your māān is in a good temper.' (Mrs. Honey.)

Later.

I went into J.'s room just now to put a book there —and turned down the pink bed-cover to see if he had enough blankets. As I did so I thought of J. as a boy of about 17. I had a sort of *prophetic vision* of doing just the same thing for my son . . . in years to come. The moment had no emotional value at all—especially as it was all drowned in the smell of roast mutting. There goes the gong: it sounds like a timid fire-alarm. But I wait until the first course is done. I wait until the chimpanzees have lapped up their little pool before I start a-nut-cracking wiv 'em.

Later.

The table was laid for two. I dined opposite a white serviette—shaped like a hand with spread fingers. Now I have dressed and am waiting for the motor. I rubbed some *genêt fleuri* on my collar just now: I look *different* —as though I were meant to be played on and not just to lie in a corner, with the bow in that slot opposite which fastens with two buttons. No! Now the bow is hanging from the peg—AT LEAST.

June: Paralysis as an idea. A pleasant one. Spinal disease. A shock. Failure of the Heart's Action. Some 'obscure' Horror. Dead before Friday. A cripple—unable to speak—My face all *deformed*, But the top and bottom of this sangwidge is a paralytic stroke—the important middle—heart failure. Well I've cut it for myself and eaten it day after day—day after day—It's an *endless* loaf. . . . And I'd like to put on quiet record that the physical pain is just not unbearable—only just not.

LOVE.
To be
read after
it has
happened.

At 4.30 to-day it did conquer me and I began, like the Tchehov students, to 'pace from corner to corner'— then up and down, up and down, and the pain *racked* me like a curse and I could hardly breathe. Then I sat down again and tried to take it quietly. But although I've an arm-chair and a fire and little table all drawn up comfortable I feel too ill to write. I could dictate I think p'raps—but write—no. Trop Malade.

I have been, in addition, waiting for A. all the afternoon. I thought, even in this storm, she'd 'blow over'. 'Hillo!' And about 100 A.s with quick deliberate steps have walked up this brick path but got no further. Plus that, I have nothing to read. Hurrah!!!

One's 'salvation' would I think be *music*. To have a 'cello again. That I must try. . . .

June 20th. The twentieth of June 1918.

C'est de la misère.

Non, pas ça exactement. Il y a quelque chose—une profonde malaise me suive comme un ombre.

Oh, why write bad French? Why write at all? 11,500 miles are so many—too many by 11,449¾ for me. [New Zealand is that distance from England.]

June 21. What is the matter with to-day? It is thin, white, as lace curtains are white, full of ugly noises (e.g. people opening the drawers of a cheap chest and trying to shut them again). All food seems stodgy and indigestible—no drink is hot enough. One looks hideous, hideous in the glass—bald as an egg—one feels swollen— and all one's clothes are tight. And everything is dusty, gritty—the cigarette ash crumbles and falls—the marigolds spill their petals over the dressing-table. In a house nearby someone is trying to tune a cheap cheap piano.

If I had a 'home' and could pull the curtains together, lock the door—burn something sweet, fast, walk round my own perfect room, soundlessly, watching the lights and the shadows—it would be *tolerable*—but living as I do in a public house—it's *très difficile*.

A few of its enormities.

1. I decided to *faire les ongles de mes pieds avant mon petit déjeuner*—and did not—from idleness.

2. The coffee was not hot: the bacon salt, and the plate shewed that it had been fried in a dirty pan.

3. I could not think of any small talk for Mrs. Honey, who seemed silent and distrait—burning with a very feeble wick. . . .

4. J.'s letter telling of all his immense difficulties—all the impossible things he *must* do before he could start his holiday left me lukewarm. It had somehow a *flat* taste—and I felt rather as tho' I'd read it curiously apart, not united.

5. A vague stomach-ache in my bath.

6. Nothing to read and too rainy to go out.

7. A. came—and did not ring. I felt she had enough of our friendship for the present. . . .

8. Very bad lunch. A small tough rissole which was no use to the functions and some rather watery gooseberries. I despise terribly English cooking.

9. Went for a walk and was caught in the wind and rain. Terribly cold and wretched.

10. The tea was not hot. I meant *not* to eat the bun but I ate it. *Over-smoked.*

Hotels.

I seem to spend half of my life arriving at strange hotels. And asking if I may go to bed immediately.

'And would you mind filling my hot-water bottle?...
Thank you; that is delicious. No, I shan't require
anything more.'

The strange door shuts upon the stranger, and then
I slip down in the sheets. Waiting for the shadows to
come out of the corners and spin their slow, slow web
over the Ugliest Wall-paper of All.

Pulmonary Tuberculosis.

The man in the room next to mine has the same
complaint as I. When I wake in the night I hear him
turning. And then he coughs. And I cough. And after
a silence I cough. And he coughs again. This goes on
for a long time. Until I feel we are like two roosters
calling to each other at false dawn. From far-away hidden farms.

Jour Maigre.

On Wednesday mornings Mrs. Honey comes into
my room as usual and pulls up the blinds and opens the
big french windows. Letting in the dancing light and
the swish of the sea and the creak of the boats lying at
anchor out in the Roads, and the sound of the lawn
mower and the smell of cut grass and syringa and the
cheeky whistle of that same blackbird.

Then she comes back to my bed and stands over me,
one hand pressed to her side, her old face puckered up

as though she had some news that she didn't know how to break gently.

''Tis a meatless day,' says she.

Pic-Nic.

When the two women in white came down to the lonely beach—*She* threw away her paint-box—and *She* threw away her note-book. Down they sat on the sand. The tide was low. Before them the weedy rocks were like some herd of shaggy beasts huddled at the pool to drink and staying there in a kind of stupor.

Then *She* went off and dabbled her legs in a pool thinking about the colour of flesh under water. And *She* crawled into a dark cave and sat there thinking about her childhood. Then they came back to the beach and flung themselves down on their bellies, hiding their heads in their arms. They looked like two swans.

Grownupedness.

Four o'clock. Is it light now at four o'clock? I jump out of bed and run over to the window. It is half-light, neither black nor blue. The wing of the coast is violet; in the lilac sky there are dark banners and little black boats manned by black shadows put out on the purple water.

Oh! how often I have watched this hour when I was a girl! But then—I stayed at the window until I grew cold—until I was icy—thrilled by something—I did not know what. Now I fly back into bed, pulling up the clothes, tucking them into my neck. And suddenly my feet find the hot-water bottle. Heavens! it is still beautifully warm. That really is thrilling.

Dame Seule.

She is little and grey, with a black velvet band round her hair, false teeth, and skinny little hands coming out of frills like the frills on cutlets.

As I passed her room one morning I saw her 'worked' brush-and-comb bag and her Common Prayer book.

Also, when she goes to the 'Ladies', for some obscure reason she wears a little shawl. . . .

At the dining-table, smiling brightly:—'This is the first time I have ever travelled alone, or stayed by myself in a Strange Hotel. But my husband does not mind. As it is so Very Quiet. Of course, if it were a Gay Place. . .' And she draws in her chin, and the bead chain rises and falls on her vanished bosom.

Remembrance.

Always, when I see foxgloves, I think of the L.'s.

Again I pass in front of their cottage, and in the window—between the daffodil curtains with the green spots—there are the great, sumptuous blooms.

'And how beautiful they are against the whitewash!' cry the L.'s.

As is their custom, when they love anything, they

make a sort of Festa. With foxgloves everywhere. And then they sit in the middle of them, like blissful prisoners, dining in an encampment of Indian Braves.

Strawberries and a Sailing Ship.

We sat on the top of the cliff overlooking the open sea. Our backs turned to the little town. Each of us had a basket of strawberries. We had just bought them from a dark woman with quick eyes—berry-finding eyes.

'They're fresh picked,' said she, 'from our own garden.'

The tips of her fingers were stained a bright red. But what strawberries! Each one was the finest—the perfect berry—the strawberry Absolute—the fruit of our childhood! The very air came fanning on straw-berry wings. And down below, in the pools, little children were bathing, with strawberry faces. . . .

Over the blue, swinging water, came a three-masted sailing-ship with nine, ten, eleven sails. Wonderfully beautiful! She came riding by as though every sail were taking its fill of the sun and the light.

And: 'Oh how I'd love to be on board!' said Anne.

(The captain was below, but the crew lay about, idle and handsome. 'Have some strawberries!' we said, slipping and sliding on the rocking decks, and shaking the baskets. They ate them in a kind of dream. . . .)

And the ship sailed on. Leaving us in a kind of dream, too. With the empty baskets. . . .

[At the beginning of July K.M. returned to Redcliffe Road. At the end of the month we moved into No. 2 Portland Villas, East Heath Road, Hampstead.]

July 5. [*47 Redcliffe Road.*] To-day, this evening, after I have come home (for I must go out and buy some fruits) commence encore une vie nouvelle. Turn over and you'll see how good I become—a different child.

Later. I have read—given way to reading—two books by Octave Mirbeau—and after them I see dreadfully and finally, (1) that the French are a filthy people, (2) that their corruption is so *puante*—I'll not go near 'em again. No, the English couldn't stoop to this. They aren't human; they are in the good old English parlance —*monkeys.*

I must start writing again. They decide me. Something must be put up against this.

Ach, Tchehov! why are you dead? Why can't I talk to you, in a big darkish room, at late evening—where the light is green from the waving trees outside. I'd like to write a series of *Heavens:* that would be one.

I must not forget my *timidity* before closed doors. My debate as to whether I shall ring too loud or not loud enough. . . . It's deep deep deep: in fact it is the 'explanation' of the failure of K.M. as a writer up to the present, and Oh! what a good *Anfang zu einer Geschichte!*

The Eternal Question.

I pose myself, yet once more, *my* Eternal Question. What is it that makes the moment of delivery so difficult for me? If I were to sit down—now—and just to write out, plain, some of the stories—all written, all ready, in my mind 'twould take me days. There are so many of them. I sit and *think* them out, and if I overcome my lassitude and *do* take the pen they ought (they are so word-perfect) to write themselves. But it's the activity. I haven't a place to write in or on—the chair isn't comfortable—yet even as I complain *this* seems the place and *this* the chair. And don't I want to write them? Lord! Lord! it's my only desire—my one *happy issue*. And only yesterday I was thinking—even my present state of health is a great gain. It makes things so rich, so important, so longed for . . . changes one's focus.

. . . When one is little and ill and far away in a remote bedroom all that happens *beyond* is marvellous. . . . Alors, I am always in that remote bedroom. Is that why I seem to see, this time in London—nothing but what is marvellous—marvellous—and incredibly beautiful?

The tide is full in the Redcliffe Road. One by one the doors have opened, have slammed shut. Now, in their blind way, the houses are fed. That poor little violin goes on, tearing up note after note—there is a strange dazzling white cloud over the houses and a pool of blue.

Evening Primrose.

'All my virtues—all my rich nature—gone,' she said, 'grown over, tangled, forgotten, deserted like a once-upon-a-time garden.' She smiled and pulled down her hat and pulled her coat together as though making ready to stumble out into it and be lost too. 'A dark place,' said she, wavering to her feet. And then she smiled again. 'Perhaps there *is* just left my—my—curiosity about myself. Evening Primrose. . . .' She half shut her eyes, stooping forward, curiously as though the plant had sprung up at her feet. 'I always did hate evening primroses. They *sound* such darlings, but when you see one they're such weedy, shabby—flower on the grave without a grave stone—sort of things—I don't mean anything symbolical by that,' said she, 'God forbid!' and was gone.

The Redcliffe Road.

Maisie—the student—their lodgers—she risks anything.
The little leaf that blows in—her memory of the park and crocodile—then there must be her cat called *Millie*. That quick *Hook on, dear girl*—and the pain so great that she almost sobs. But nothing happens—

> Nay, though my heart should break,
> I would not bind you.

Miss Ruddick who always plays with her music propped against the towel rail, and whenever she pulls out her handkerchief out comes an end of resin gummed on a flannel as well.

On these summer evenings the sound of the steps along the street is quite different. They knock-knock-knock along, but lightly and easily, as though they belonged to people who were walking home at their ease, after a procession or a pic-nic or a day at the sea.

The sky is pale and clear: the silly piano is overcome and reels out waltzes—old waltzes, spinning, drunk with sentiment—gorged with memory.

This is the hour when the poor underfed dog appears, at a run, nosing the dry gutter. He is so thin that his body is like a cage on four wooden pegs. . . . His lean triangle of a head is down, his long straight tail is out, and up and down, up and down he goes, silent and fearfully eager. The street watches him from its creeper-covered balconies, from its open windows—but the fat lady on the ground floor who is no better than she should be comes out, down the steps to the gate, with a bone. His tail, as he waits for her to give it him, bangs against the gate-post, like a broom-handle—and the street says she's a fool to go feeding strange dogs. Now she'll never be rid of him.

(What I'd like to convey is that, at this hour, with this half light and the pianos and the open, empty sounding houses, he is the spirit of the street—running up and down, poor dog, when he ought to have been done away with years ago.)

The Middle of the Note.

Whenever I have a conversation about Art which is more or less interesting I begin to wish to God I could destroy all that I have written and start again: it all seems like so many 'false starts'. Musically speaking, it is not—has not been—in the middle of the note—you know what I mean? When, on a cold morning perhaps, you've been playing and it has sounded all right—until suddenly, you *realize* you are warm—you have only just begun to play. Oh, how badly this is expressed! How confused and even ungrammatical!

Now the day was divine—warm, soft sunshine lay upon her arms and breast like velvet—tiny clouds, silver ones, shone upon the dazzling blue—the garden trees were full of gold light—and a strange brightness came from the houses—from the open windows with their fairy curtains and flower-pots . . . the white steps and the narrow spiked railings.

Inconsequence.

'Did M. wear a grey dressing-gown with a dark red piping?' she asked.

'No, he was dressed.'

'Oh! Then I suppose he was *very* dressed; he always is.'

That made her think, suddenly, of another friend of his—a young, fattish man who wore spectacles and was extremely serious, with a kind of special fatness that she had noticed went with just that kind of seriousness. She saw him standing by a wash-table drying his neck—and she saw his hair right to the neck-band of his shirt. His hair was, as usual, too long.

'How awful S. must be without a collar!'

'Without a collar?' He looked at her; he almost gasped.

'Yes, in a shirt and trousers.'

'In a shirt and trousers!' he exclaimed. 'I've never seen him in one—'

'No—but— Oh, well—'

He positively fixed her at that.

'How *extraordinarily* inconsequential you are!'

And all in a minute she was laughing.

'Well,' she said, 'men are . . .'

And she looked out of the window at the tall poplar, with its whispering leaves, with its beautiful top, gold in the last sunlight.

On the wall of the kitchen there was a shadow, shaped like a little mask with two gold slits for eyes. It danced up and down.

August 2nd. 2 Portland Villas, Hampstead. Her heart had not spoken. . . . When it does—too late—the pain of it. I ought to have felt like this—often, often. . . .

September 20th. My fits of temper are really terrifying. I had one this (Sunday) morning and tore a page up of the book I was reading—and absolutely lost my head.

Very significant. When it was over J. came in and stared. 'What is the matter? What have you done? Why? You look *all dark*.' He drew back the curtains and called it an effect of light, but when I came into my studio to dress I saw it was not that. I was a deep earthy colour, *with pinched eyes*. Strangely enough these fits are L. and F. over again. I am more like L. than anybody. We are *unthinkably* alike, in fact.

It is a dark, reluctant day. The fire makes a noise like a flag—and there is the familiar sound from below of someone filling buckets. I am very stiff, very unused to writing now, and yet, as I sit here, it's as though my dear one, my ONLY one, came and sat down opposite me and gazed at me across the table. And I think suddenly of the verses which seemed so awfully good in my girlhood.

> Others leave me—all things leave me,
> You remain.

My room really has for me a touch of fairy. Is there anything better than my room? Anything outside? The kitten says not—but then it's such a hunting-ground for the kitten; the sun throws the shape of the window on to the carpet, and in those four little square fields the silly flies wander, ever so spied upon by the little lion under the *sommier* frill. . . .

Oh dear—Oh dear—where are my people? With whom have I been happiest? With nobody in particular. It has all been mush of a mushness.

DEATH OF A KITTEN

Later. That kitten took sick, was taken away, lived two weeks in great torture, then for two days it lost the will to live. It became just a cotton reel of fur with two great tearful eyes: 'Why has this happened to me?' So the vet. killed it. It had gastric trouble, acute constipation, with a distended belly, and canker in both ears. The two days before it went away it suffered here. I bought it a ball and it tried to play a little—but no! It couldn't even wash itself. It came up to me, stood on its hind legs, opened its little jaws and *tried* to mew. No sound came; I never saw anything more pitiful.

September 30. I hope this pen works. Yes, it does.

The last day in September—*immensely* cold, a kind of solid cold outside the windows. My fire has played traitor nearly all day, and I have been, in the good, old-fashioned way, feeling my skin *curl*.

Don't read this. Do you hear that train whistle and now the leaves—the dry leaves—and now the fire—fluttering and breaking.

Why *doesn't* she bring the lamps?

October 21. L.M. is going to town. I must take some of my dear money out of the Bank and give it her. I am in bed; I feel very sick. Queer altogether—decomposing a bit. It's a pale, silent day: I would like to be walking in a wood, far away.

Health seems to me now more remote than anything —unattainable. Best to stay in bed and be horrid from there. This sky in waves of blue and cream and grey is like the sky overhanging a dead calm sea, when you hear someone rowing, far, far away; and then the voices from the boat and the rattle of the chain and the barking of the ship's dog all sound loud. There is as usual a smell of onions and chop bones in the house.

What do I want her to buy for me? When it really becomes an urgent matter—I want *nothing*—waste of money—I feel like Mlle. Séguin, who wouldn't hang the pictures in her new flat because *Life is such a breath, little Dolly.*

October. Hampstead. I ought to write something brief for the *Nation* to-day and earn a bit more money, a 'Little Lunch at the Club' or something of that kind. It's not difficult; in fact it is too easy for me because if I do err more on one side than t'other—I'm over-fluent.

This view from the window is simply superb—the pale sky and the half-bare trees. It's so beautiful it might be the country—*Russian* country as *I* see it.

I never connected until to-day—*sang froid* with Cold blood. This is a word which is one of New Zealand's queer 'uns, like calling the Savoy the Sāvoy—or talking of the aryeighted bread shops. Sagn freūd.

October 24. This is simply the most *Divine Spot*. So remote, so peaceful; full of colour, full of Autumn; the sunset is real, and the sound of somebody splitting small wood is real, too. If only one could live up here for really a long time and not have to see anybody. . . . It might very well be France, it's much more like France than it is like England.

> The place—remote—the dresses and scarves old;
> The year—fruitful! their talk and laughter gay.

The Ladies' Club in Wartime.

Ladies to the Centre: A round hall, very dim, lighted from above. A loud, reluctant (swing-glass) door that can't bear people trying to burst their way in and loathes people trying to burst their way out. To one side of the door the porter's cave dotted with pigeon-holes, and a desk, furnished with a telephone, usually a big tea-stained china tea cup crowned with its saucer. In front of it a squeaking revolving chair with a torn imitation-leather seat.

Good night.

And once again the door opened, and she passed as it were into another world—the world of night, cold, timeless, inscrutable.

Again she saw the beautiful fall of the steps, the dark garden edged with fluttering ivy—on the other side of the road the huge bare willows—and above them the sky big and bright with stars.

Again there came that silence that was a question—but this time she did not hesitate. She moved forward, very softly and gently—as though fearful of making a ripple in that boundless pool of quiet. She put her arm round her friend. The friend is astonished—murmurs 'It has been so nice.' The other—'Good night, *dear friend.*' A long tender embrace. Yes, that was it—of course that was what was wanting.

The Blow.

'I'—like a blow on her heart—'I have come—for ...'
She leaned against the door, quite faint.
'Yes?' said she.
'This—' tightly, quickly, he caught her up into his arms.

The Fly.

December 31. 4.45 p.m. Oh, the times when she had walked upside-down on the ceiling, run up glittering panes, floated on a lake of light, flashed through a shining beam!

And God looked upon the fly fallen into the jug of milk and saw that it was good. And the smallest Cherubim and Seraphim of all, who delight in misfortune, struck their silver harps and shrilled: 'How is the fly fallen, fallen!'

JANUARY 1. J. CAME TO BED AT TEN MINUTES
to twelve. Said he: 'Don't go to sleep before the New
Year.' I lay holding my watch. I think I did go to sleep
for a moment. The window was wide open and I looked
out and over a big soft hollow, with a sprinkle of lights
between. Then the hour struck: the bells rang—hooter,
sirens, horns, trumpets sounded. The church organ
pealed out (reminding me of Hans Andersen) and an
Australian called *Coo—ee* (I longed to reply). I wanted
L.M. to hear and to see. I called loudly to her ever so
many times, but she had 'chosen' to take a bath. . . .

May 19. 6 p.m. I wish I had some idea of how old this
notebook is. The writing is very faint and far away.
Now it is May 1919. Six o'clock. I am sitting in my
own room thinking of Mother: I want to cry. But my
thoughts are beautiful and full of gaiety. I think of *our*
house, *our* garden, *us* children—the lawn, the gate, and
Mother coming in. 'Children! Children!' I really only ask
for time to write it all—time to write my books. Then I
don't mind dying. I live to write. The lovely world
(God, how lovely the external world is!) is there and I
bathe in it and am refreshed. But I feel as though I had
a DUTY, someone has set me a task which I am bound to
finish. Let me finish it: let me finish it without hurrying—leaving all as fair as I can. . . .

My little Mother, my star, my courage, my *own*.
I seem to dwell in her now. We live in *the same world*.

Not quite this world, not quite another. I do not care for people: and the idea of fame, of being a success—that's nothing, less than nothing. I love my family and a few others dearly, and I love, in the old—in the ancient way, through and through, my husband.

Not a soul knows where she is. She goes slowly, thinking it all over, wondering how she can express it *as she wants to*—asking for time and for peace.

Escape.

She was sure I would be cold, and as usual tried to make of my departure une petite affaire sérieuse. I always try to thieve out, steal out. I should like to let myself down from a window, or just withdraw like a ray of light.

'Are you sure you won't have your cape ... etc., etc., etc.?'

Her attitude made me quite sure. I went out. At the corner the flying, gay, eager wind ran at me. It was too much to bear. I went on for a yard or two, shivering—then I came home. I slipped the Yale key into the lock like a thief, shut the door *dead* quiet. Up she came, up the stairs.

'So it *was* too cold, after all!'

I couldn't answer or even look at her. I had to turn my back and pull off my gloves. Said she:

'I have a blouse-pattern here I want to show you.'

At that I crept upstairs, came into my room, and shut the door. It was a miracle she did not follow. . . .

What is there in all this to make me HATE her so? What do you see? She has known me try to get in and out without anyone knowing it dozens of times—that is true. I have even *torn* my heart out and told her how it hurts my last little defences to be questioned—how it makes me feel just for the moment an independent being, to be allowed to go and come unquestioned. But that is just 'Katie's funniness. She doesn't mean it, of course. . . .'

We hardly spoke at lunch. When it was over she asked me again if she might show me the pattern. I felt so ill, it seemed to me that even a hen could see at a side-glance of its little leaden eye how ill I felt. I don't remember what I said. But in she came and put before me—something. Really, I hardly know what it was. 'Let the little dressmaker help you,' I said. But there was nothing to say.

She murmured: 'Purple chiffon front neck sleeves.' I don't know. Finally I asked her to take it away.

'What *is* it, Katie? Am I interrupting your work?'

'Yes, we'll call it that.'

Being Alone.

Saturday: This joy of being alone. What is it? I feel so gay and at peace—the whole house takes the air. Lunch is ready. I have a baked egg, apricots and cream, cheese straws and black coffee. How delicious! A baby meal! Mother shares it with me. Athenæum is asleep and then awake on the studio sofa. He has a silver spoon of cream—then hides under the sofa frill and puts out a paw for my finger. I gather the dried leaves from the plant in the big white bowl, and because I *must* play with something, I take an orange up to my room and throw it and catch it as I walk up and down. . . .

[This note appears later, re-written, in the following form.]

Saturday. Peaceful and gay. The whole house takes the air. Athenæum is asleep and then awake on the studio sofa. He has a silver spoonful of my cream at lunch-time—then hides under the sofa frill and plays the game of the Darting Paw. I gather the dried leaves from the plant in the big white bowl; they are powdered with silver. There is nobody in the house, and yet whose is this faint whispering? On the stairs there are tiny spots of gold—tiny footprints. . . .

Geraniums.

The red geraniums have bought the garden over my head. They are there, established, back in the old home, every leaf and flower unpacked and in its place—and quite determined that no power on earth will ever move them again. Well, *that* I don't mind. But why should they make me feel a stranger? Why should they ask me every time I go near: 'And what are you doing in a London garden?' They burn with arrogance and pride. And I am the little Colonial walking in the London garden patch—allowed to look, perhaps, but not to linger. If I lie on the grass they positively shout at me: 'Look at her, lying on *our* grass, pretending she lives here, pretending this is her garden, and that tall back of the house, with the windows open and the coloured curtains lifting, is her house. She is a stranger—an alien. She is nothing but a little girl sitting on the Tinakori hills and dreaming: "I went to London and married an Englishman, and we lived in a tall grave house with red geraniums and white daisies in the garden at the back." *Im*-pudence!'

[This note appears later, re-written, in the following form.]

The red geraniums have bought the garden over my head and taken possession. They are settled in, every leaf and flower unpacked and in its place, and never do they mean to move again! Well—that I could bear. But why because I've let them in should they throw me out? They won't even let me lie on the grass without their shouting: '*Im*-pudence!'

A Dream.

Sometimes I glance up at the clock. Then I know I am expecting Chummie. The bell peals. I run out on to the landing. I hear his hat and stick thrown on to the hall table. He runs up the stairs, three at a time. 'Hullo, darling!' But I can't move—I can't move. He puts his arm round me, holding me tightly, and we kiss—a long, firm, family kiss. And the kiss means: We are of the same blood; we have absolute confidence in each other; we love; all is well; nothing can ever come between us.

We come into my room. He goes over to the glass. 'By Jove, I am hot.' Yes, he is very hot. A deep childish colour shows in his cheeks, his eyes are brilliant, his lips burn, he strokes the hair back from his forehead with the palm of his hand. I pull the curtains together and the room is shadowy. He flings himself down on the sommier and lights a cigarette, and watches the smoke, rising so slowly.

'Is that better?' I ask.

'Perfect, darling—simply perfect. The light reminds me of . . .'

And then the dream is over and I begin working again.

England.

The two brothers were on one side of the room, I on the other. R. sat on the floor inclined towards J. J. lay on the stickle-back, very idly.

'If you could have your wish, where would you be?'

First he thought a café in some foreign town . . . in Spain . . . no, in Grenoble, perhaps . . . sitting listening to music and watching the people. We are just passing through. . . . There is a lake and a river near. . . . But then, NO. A farmhouse in Sussex—some good old furniture—knocking about in the garden—rolling the lawn, perhaps—yes, rolling the lawn. An infant—two good servants. And then, when it grew dark—to go in, have some milk, then I go to my study and you to yours and work for about an hour and a half and then trundle off to bed. I would like to earn my living, but *not* by writing. I feel that my talent as a writer isn't a great one—I'll have to be careful of it. . . . Yes, that's what I'd like. No new places—no new things. I don't *want* them. Would you like that?

I felt his brother was with him, the brother inclined towards him, understanding and sharing that life—the homestead on the Downs—his English country—the sober quiet. . . .

'Would you like that?'

No, I don't want that. No, I don't want England. England is of no use to me. What do I mean by that? I mean there never has been—never will be—any rapprochement between us, *never*. . . . The lack of its *appeal*—that is what I chiefly hate. I would not care if I never saw the English country again. Even in its flowering I feel deeply antagonistic to it, and I will never change.

A Good Beginning.

May 30. First comes L.M. I give her orders. Ask her to supervise the maid till Monday. 'Be gentle with her: help her to make the beds; and just tell her how everything must be.' Then in detail I sketch out the maid's programme. 'Send Ralph, please.' Ralph arrives. I arrange the food. Then settle all that must be done, coercing Ralph, putting her mind in order if I can, making her see the bright side of things, sending her away (I hope) feeling important and happy.

I go upstairs to see Maud, to say good morning, to hope 'she will be happy'. 'Just take things gently; I'll quite understand that you can't get into our ways at once. Ask Miss B. and the cook for what you want. But if you wish to see me, don't hesitate to come in. I was so glad you were early.' She was very reassured. Her eyes shone (she's only a little girl). She said it was like the country. As she walked up from the tram the birds sang 'something beautiful'. This instead of the 'long drag up the hill' was cheering. I left her happy. I know I did.

Downstairs just to say Good day to Mrs. Moody and to say there were some flowers for her to take home. The good creature was on her knees polishing and saying it was such a fine day. Bless her 60 years! We had a little joke or two and I came away.

L.M. again—just for a moment to say: 'As you have a machine, don't hem dusters by hand as I see you are doing. Keep your energies for something *important!*'

Then I sit down to work, and there comes a steady, pleasant vibration from the ship. If only I could always control these four women like this! I must learn to.

May 31. *Work.* Shall I be able to express one day my love of work—my desire to be a better writer—my longing to take greater pains. And the passion I feel. It takes the place of religion—it *is* my religion—of people

—I create my people: of 'life'—it *is* Life. The temptation is to kneel before it, to adore, to prostrate myself, to stay too long in a state of ecstasy before the *idea* of it. I must be more busy about my master's business.

Oh, God! The sky is filled with the sun, and the sun is like music. The sky is full of music. Music comes streaming down these great beams. The wind touches the harp-like trees, shakes little jets of music—little shakes, little trills from the flowers. The shape of every flower is like a sound. My hands open like five petals. Praise Him! Praise Him! No, I am overcome; I am dazed; it is too much to bear.

A little fly has dropped by mistake into the huge sweet cup of a magnolia. Isaiah (or was it Elisha?) was caught up into Heaven in a chariot of fire *once*. But when the weather is divine and I am free to work, such a journey is positively nothing.

The Angel of Mercy.
May. The day the housemaid had to leave because her husband 'didn't want her to work no more' and, to consolidate his authority, had punched her so hard in the neck that she had a great red swelling under her ear, the cook became a kind of infallible being—an angel of mercy. Nothing was too much for her. Stairs were rays of light up which she floated. She wore her cap differently: it gave her the air of a hospital nurse. Her voice changed. She suggested puddings as though they were compresses: whiting, because they were so 'delicate

and harmless'. Trust me! Lean on me! There is nothing I cannot do! was her attitude. Every time she left me, she left me for her mysterious reasons—to lay out the body again and again—to change the stiffened hand—to pull the paper frill over the ominous spot appearing.

The Cook.

The cook is evil. After lunch I trembled so that I had to lie down on the sommier—thinking about her. I meant—when she came up to see me—to say *so much* that she'd have to go. I waited, playing with the wild kitten. When she came, I said it all, and more, and *she* said how sorry she was and agreed and apologized and quite understood. She stayed at the door, plucking at a doily. 'Well, I'll see it doesn't happen in future. I *quite* see what you mean.'

So the serpent still slept between us. Oh! why won't she turn and speak her mind? This pretence of being fond of me! I believe she thinks she is. There is something in what L.M. says: she is not consciously evil. She is a FOOL, of course. I have to do all the managing and all the explaining. I have to cook everything before she cooks it. I believe she thinks she is a treasure . . . no, wants to think it. At bottom she knows her corruptness. There are moments when it comes to the surface, comes out, like a stain, in her face. Then her eyes are like the eyes of a woman-prisoner—a creature looking up as you enter her cell and saying: 'If you'd known what a hard life I've had you wouldn't be surprised to see me here.'

[This appears again in the following form.]

Cook to See Me.

    As I opened the door, I saw her sitting in the middle of the room, hunched, still. . . . She got up, obedient, like a prisoner when you enter a cell. And her eyes said, as a prisoner's eyes say, 'Knowing the life I've had, I'm the last to be surprised at finding myself here.'

The Cook's Story.

    Her first husband was a pawnbroker. He learned his trade from her uncle, with whom she lived, and was more like her big brother than anything else from the age of thirteen. After he had married her they prospered. He made a perfect pet of her—they used to say. His sisters put it that he made a perfect fool of himself over her. When their children were fifteen and nine he urged his employers to take a man into their firm—a great friend of his—and persuaded them; really went security for this man. When she saw the man she went all over cold. She said, 'Mark me, you've not done right: no good will come of this.' But he laughed it off. Time passed: the man proved a villain. When they came to take stock, they found all the stock was false: he'd sold everything. This preyed on her husband's mind, went on preying, kept him up at night, made a changed man of him, he went mad as you might say over figures, worrying. One evening, sitting in his chair, very late, he *died* of a clot of blood on the brain.

She was left. Her big boy was old enough to go out, but the little one was still not more than a baby: he was so nervous and delicate. The doctors had never let him go to school.

One day her brother-in-law came to see her and advised her to sell up her home and get some work. 'All that keeps you back,' he said, 'is little Bert. Now, I'd advise you to place a certain sum with your solicitor for him and put him out—in the country.' He said he'd take him. I did as he advised. But, funny! I never heard a word from the child after he'd gone. I used to ask why he didn't write, and they said, when he can write a decent letter you shall have it—not before. That went on for a twelvemonth, and I found afterwards he'd been writing all the time, grieving to be took away, and they'd never sent his letters. Then quite sudden his uncle wrote and said he must be taken away. He'd done the most awful things—things I couldn't find you a name for—he'd turned *vicious*—he was a little criminal! What his uncle said was I'd spoiled the child and he was going to make a man of him, and he'd beaten him and half starved him and when he was frightened at night and screamed, he turned him out into the New Forest and made him sleep under the branches. My big boy went down to see him. 'Mother,' he says, 'you wouldn't know little Bert. He can't speak. He won't come near anybody. He starts off if you touch him; he's like a little beast.' And, oh dear, the things he'd done! Well, you hear of people doing those things before they're put into orphanages. But when I heard that and thought it was the same little baby his father used to carry into Regent's Park bathed and dressed of a Sunday morning—well, I felt my religion was going from me.

I had a terrible time trying to get him into an orphanage. I begged for three months before they would take him. Then he was sent to Bisley. But after I'd been to see him there, in his funny clothes and all—I could see 'is misery. I was in a nice place at the time, cook to a butcher in a large way in Kensington, but that poor child's eyes—they used to follow me—and a sort of shivering that came over him when people went near.

Well, I had a friend that kept a boarding house in Kensington. I used to visit her, and a friend of hers, a big well-set-up fellow, quite the gentleman, an engineer who worked in a garage, came there very often. She used to joke and say he wanted to walk me out. I laughed it off till one day she was very serious. She said, 'You're a very silly woman. He earns good money; he'd give you a home and you could have your little boy.' Well, he was to speak to me next day and I made up my mind to listen. Well, he did, and he couldn't have put it nicer. 'I can't give you a house to start with,' he said, 'but you shall have three good rooms and the kid, and I'm earning good money and shall be more.'

A week after, he come to me. 'I can't give you any money this week,' he says, 'there's things to pay for from when I was single. But I daresay you've got a bit put by.' And I was a fool, you know, I didn't think it funny. 'Oh yes,' I said, 'I'll manage.' Well, so it went on for three weeks. We'd arranged not to have little Bert for a month because, he said, he wanted me to himself, and he was so fond of him. A big fellow, he used to cling to me like a child and call me mother.

After three weeks was up I hadn't a penny. I'd been taking my jewels and best clothes to put away to pay for him until he was straight. But one night I said, 'Where's my money?' He just up and gave me such a smack in the face I thought my head would burst. And that began it. Every time I asked him for money he beat me. As I said, I was very religious at the time, used to wear a crucifix under my clothes and couldn't go to bed without kneeling by the side and saying my prayers—no, not even the first week of my marriage. Well, I went to a clergyman and told him everything and he said, 'My child,' he said, 'I am very sorry for you, but with God's help,' he said, 'it's your duty to make him a better man. You say your first husband was so good. Well, perhaps God has kept this trial for you until now.' I went home—and that very night he tore my crucifix off and hit me on the head when I knelt down. He said he wouldn't have me say my prayers; it made him wild. I had a little dog at the time I was very fond of, and he used to pick it up and shout, 'I'll teach it to say its prayers,' and beat it before my eyes—until—well, such was the man he was.

Then one night he came in the worse for drink and fouled the bed. I couldn't stand it. I began to cry. He gave me a hit on the ear and I fell down, striking my head on the fender. When I came to, he was gone. I ran out into the street just as I was—I ran as fast as I could, not knowing where I was going—just dazed—my nerves were gone. And a lady found me and took me to her home and I was there three weeks. And after that I never went back. I never even told my people. I found work, and not till months after I went to see my sister. 'Good gracious!' she says, 'we all thought you was murdered!' And I never see him since. . . .

Those were dreadful times. I was so ill, I could scarcely hardly work and of course I couldn't get my little boy out. He had to grow up in it. And so I had to start all over again. I had nothing of his, nothing of mine. I lost it all except my marriage lines. Somehow I remembered them just as I was running out that night and put them in my boddy—sort of an instinct as you might say.

J. digs the garden as though he were exhuming a hated body or making a hole for a loved one.

The ardent creature spent more than half her time in church praying to be delivered from temptation. But God grew impatient at last and caused the door to be shut against her. 'For Heaven's sake,' said he, 'give the temptation a chance!'

It's raining, but the air is soft, smoky, warm. Big drops patter on the languid leaves, the tobacco flowers lean over. Now there is a rustle in the ivy. Wingley has appeared from the garden next door; he bounds from the wall. And delicately, lifting his paws, pointing his ears, very afraid that big wave will overtake him, he wades over the lake of green grass.

'Mr. Despondency's daughter, Muchafraid, went through the water singing.'

She said: 'I don't feel in the least afraid. I feel like a little rock that the rising tide is going to cover. You won't be able to see me ... big waves ... but they'll go down again. I shall be there—winking bright.'

Oh, what sentimental toshery!

June 10. I have discovered that I cannot burn the candle at one end and write a book with the other.

Life without *work*—I would commit suicide. Therefore work is more important than life.

June 21. Bateson and his love of the louse for its own sake. Pedigree lice. £100 a year from the Royal Institute: a large family: desperately poor: but he never notices. The lives he saved in the Balkan war with shaving and

Thymol. Cases reduced from 7000 to 700. No reward, not even an O.B.E. He dissects them, finds their glands and so on, keeps them in tiny boxes; they feed on his arm. The louse and the bed-bug.

Hydatids: the Australian who got them: handfuls of immature grapes. They attack the liver. In the human body they reproduce indefinitely. When they are passed and a sheep is attacked by them, they develop *hooks* and become long worms.

The Egyptian disease: a parasite which attacks the veins and arteries and causes fluxion—constant bleeding. It is another egg drunk in water. After it has been in man the only thing it can affect is a water-snail. It goes through an entirely new cycle of *being* until it can attack man again.

Dysentery: another parasite.

Hydrophobia: the virus from the dog is taken and a rabbit is infected. That rabbit is used to infect another rabbit: the 2nd a 3rd, and so on, until you get a rabbit who is practically *pure* virus. The spinal cords are then taken from these rabbits and dried by a vacuum. The result is pounded up fine into an emulsion: 1st rabbit, 2nd rabbit, 3rd rabbit, etc., and the patient is injected progressively till at last he receives a dose which, if he had not been prepared to resist it, would kill him outright. The disease develops very slowly; the treatment is very expensive. Symptoms are a profuse shiny bubbling saliva, and gasping and groaning as in gas-poisoning. No barking, no going on all fours.

In lockjaw the jaw does not lock.

Pasteur was a very dreamer of dreamers. Human beings are a *side-line* to science.

All this I talked over with Sorapure, June 21. His point of view about medicine seems to me *just completely right*. I'd willingly let him take off my head, look inside, and pop it on again, if he thought it might assist future generations. Quite the right man to have at one's dying bedside. He'd get me at any rate so interested in the process—gradual loss of sensitiveness, coldness in the joints, etc.—I'd lie there thinking: this is very valuable to know; I must make a note of this.

As he stood at the door talking: 'Nothing is incurable; it's all a question of *time*. What seems so useless to-day may be just that link which will make all plain to a future generation. . . .' I had a sense of the *larger breath*, of the mysterious lives within lives, and the Egyptian parasite beginning its new cycle of being in a water-snail affected me like a *great* work of art. No, that's not what I mean. It made me feel how *perfect* the world is, with its worms and hooks and ova, how incredibly perfect. There is the sky and the sea and the shape of a lily, and there is all this other as well. The *balance* how perfect! (*Salut*, Tchehov!) I would not have the one without the other.

The clocks are striking ten. Here in my room the sky looks lilac; in the bath-room it is like the skin of a peach. Girls are laughing.

I have consumption. There is still a great deal of

moisture (*and* pain) in my BAD lung. But I do not care.
I do not want anything I could not have. Peace,
solitude, time to write my books, beautiful external
life to watch and ponder—no more. O, I'd like a child
as well—a baby boy; *mais je demande trop!*

[Part of this note appears again in the following form.]

As he stood at the door he said quietly, 'Nothing is
incurable. What seems so useless to-day may be the
link that will make all plain to-morrow.' We had been
discussing hydatids, the Egyptian parasite that begins
its cycle of existence being in a water-snail and the
effects of hydrophobia. He smiled gently. There was
nothing to be alarmed or shocked or surprised at. It
was all a question of knowing these things as they should
be known and not otherwise. But he said none of this
and went off to his next case. . . .

At breakfast time a mosquito and a wasp came to the
edge of the honey dish to drink. The mosquito was a
lovely little high-stepping gazelle, but the wasp was a
fierce roaring tiger. Drink, my darlings!

When the coffee is cold L.M. says: These things
have to happen sometimes. And she looks mysterious
and important, as if, as a matter of fact, she had known
all along that this was a cold-coffee day.

What I felt was, he said, that I wasn't in the whole

of myself at all. I'd got locked in, somehow, in some little ... top room in my mind, and strangers had got in—people I'd never seen before were making free of the rest of it. There was a dreadful feeling of confusion, chiefly that, and ... vague noises—like things being moved—changed about—in my head. I lit the candle and sat up and in the mirror I saw a dark, brooding, strangely lengthened face.

'The feeling roused by the cause is more important than the cause itself. ...' That is the kind of thing I like to say to myself as I get into the train. And then, as one settles into the corner—'For example'—or 'Take —for instance ...' It's a good game for *one*.

She fastens on a white veil and hardly knows herself. Is it becoming or is it not becoming? Ah, who is there to say. There is a lace butterfly on her left cheek and a spray of flowers on her right. Two dark bold eyes stare through the mesh—Surely not hers. Her lips tremble; faint, she sinks on her bed. And now she doesn't want to go. Must she? She is being driven out of the flat by those bold eyes. Out you go. Ah, how cruel! (*Second Violin.*)

But her hand is large and cold with big knuckles and short square nails. It is not a little velvet hand that sighs, that yields—faints dead away and has to be revived again only to faint once more. (*S.V.*)

What do I want? she thought. What do I really want more than anything else in the world? If I had a wishing ring or Ali Baba's lamp—no, it wasn't Ali Baba—it was—Oh, what did it matter! Just supposing someone came. . . . 'I am here to grant your dearest wish.' And she saw, vaguely, a fluffy little creature with a silver paper star on a wand—a school fairy. . . . What should I say? It was cold in the kitchen, cold and dim. The tap dripped slowly, as tho' the water were half frozen. . . . (*S.V.*)

Miss Todd and Miss Hopper were second violins. Miss Bray was a viola.

Midday strikes on various bells—some velvety soft, some languid, some regretful, and one impatient—a youthful bell ringing high and quick above the rest. He thought joyfully: That's the bell for me! . . .

Cinderella.

Oh, my sisters—my beautiful Peacock-proud sisters—have pity on me as I sit with my little broom beside the cold ashes while you dance at the Prince's party. But why—is the Fairy Godmother, the coach, the plumes and glass slippers just –faery—and all the rest of the story deeply, deeply true? Fate I suppose—Fate. It had to be. These things happen so. La réponse: Poor old girl –of course she is awfully sorry for her, but she does become a bore—doesn't she? There's no getting away from it.

When they got into bed together her feet rushed to greet his like little puppies that had been separated all day from their brothers. And first they chased one another and played and nudged gently. But then, they settled down, curled up, twined together under the clothes (like puppies on a warm hearth-rug) and went to sleep.

Dark Bogey is a little inclined to jump into the milk-jug to rescue the fly.

Fairylike, the fire rose in two branched flames like the golden antlers of some enchanted stag.

So he sat there, burning the letters, and each time he cast a fresh packet on the flame, his shadow, immense, huge, leapt out of the wall opposite him. It looked, sitting so stiff and straight, like some horrible old god, toasting his knees at the flames of the sacrifice.

Two Climates.

I'd always rather be in a place that is too hot rather than one that's too cold. But I'd always rather be with people who loved me too little rather than with people who loved me too much.

'She has made her bed,' said Belle—'she must lie on it.' I reflected thankfully that in this case that would be no hardship—on the contrary, indeed. I hoped it was what they were both longing to do. . . .

North Africa. The whole valley is smothered in little white lilies. You never saw such a sight! They make me feel so wretchedly homesick. They smell just like dear old Selfridge's.

Souvent j'ai dit à mon mari: Nous en prenons un? Et il me dit: Ah, non, non, ma pauvre femme. Notre petit moment pour jouer est passé. Je ne peux rien faire que de rester dans une chaise en faisant des grimaces, et ça fait trembler plus que ça ne fait rire un petit enfant.

When I read Dr. Johnson, I feel like a little girl sitting at the same table. My eyes grow round. I don't only listen; I take him in *immensely*.

'Don't you think it would be marvellous,' she said, 'to have just one person in one's life to whom one could tell everything?' She leant forward, put down her cup, but stayed bent forward touching the spoon against the saucer. She looked up—'Or is it just childish of me— just absurd to want such a thing? . . . All the same,' she leaned back, smiling, 'childish or not—how wonderful it would be—how wonderful! to feel—from this person, this one person—I really don't need to hide anything. It would be such heavenly happiness!' she cried, suddenly, 'it would make life so . . .' she got up, went to the window, looked out vaguely and turned round again. She laughed. 'It's a queer thing,' she said, 'I've

always believed in the possibility—and yet—in reality...
Take R. and me, for instance.' And here she flung back
in a chair and leant back, still she was laughing but her
body leant to the chair as though exhausted. 'I tell him
everything. You know we're ... rather different from
most people. What I mean is—don't laugh—we love
each other simply tremendously—we're everything to
each other! In fact he's the one person on earth for me
—and yet,' and she shut her eyes and bit her lip as
though she wanted to stop laughing herself: 'try, try,
try as I can—there's always just one secret—just one—
that never can be told—that mocks me.' And then for
a moment she lay still. ...

Indoo Weather: A Dream.

'It's what you might call indoo weather,' said the
little man.

'Oh, really. ... Why that?' said I, vaguely.

He did not answer. The two polished knobs of his
behind shone as he leaned over feeding the black seams
of the boat with a brown twist.

The day was dull, steaming; there was a blackness
out at sea; the heavy waves came tolling. On the sea
grasses the large bright dew fell not. The little man's
hammer went tap-tap.

L.M. snorted, threw up her head, stamped her feet
on the wet sand, scrambled to a boulder, tore at some
sea-poppies, dug them in her hat, held the hat away,
looked, scornful, wrenched them out again.

I looked and felt vague as a king.

'Spades and buckets is round the point with the lobster catch.' The hammer tapped. He explained that all the lovers would be sent away alive in sacks if they were not given a sharp *stang* with one of these. It was an ordinary grey and red garden trowel. L.M. went off to save their lives, but not joyfully. She walked heavy, her head down, beating the trowel against her side.

We were alone. The watcher appeared. He stood always in profile, his felt hat turned up at the side, a patch on the eye nearest us. His curved pipe fell from his jaws.

'Hi, Missy,' he shouted to me. 'Why don't you give us a bit of a show out there?'

The little man remonstrated. The sea was like a mass of half-set jelly. On the horizon it seemed ages fell.

'Come on, Missy!' bawled the watcher. I took off my clothes, stepped to the edge and was drawn in. I tried to catch the stumps of an old wharf, but slime filled my nails and I was sucked out. They watched.

Suddenly there came, winnowing landward, an enormous skinny skeleton of a Hindoo, standing upright. A tattered pink and white print coat flapped about his stiff outstretched arms. He had cloth of the same with a fringe of spangles over his head. He stood upright because of the immense sweeping broom of wood growing waist-high. 'Help! Help!' I called.

The noise of the hammer came, and I felt the

watcher's patched profile. A huge unbreakable wave lifted him, tipped him near. His shadow lay even, on the surface of the dusty water—a squat head and two giant arms. It broadened into a smile.

Strangers.

I saw S. as a little fair man with a walrus moustache, a bowler much too small for him and an ancient frock coat that he keeps buttoning and unbuttoning. D.B. saw him as a grave gentleman with big black whiskers. Anyhow, there he was at the end of a dark tunnel, either coming towards us or walking away.... That started us on a fascinating subject. There are the people in D.B.'s life I've never seen (very few) and the immense number in mine that he has only heard of. What did they look like to us? And then, before we meet anyone while they are still far too far off to be seen we begin to build an image... how true is it? It's queer how well one gets to know this stranger; how often you've watched him before the other comes to take his place. ... I can even imagine someone keeping their 'first impression'—*in spite of* the other.

July.

TEDIOUS BRIEF ADVENTURE OF K.M.

A Doctor who came from Jamaica
Said: 'This time I'll mend her or break her.
I'll plug her with serum;
And if she can't bear 'em
I'll call in the next undertaker.'

MRS. NIGHTINGALE

His *locum tenens*, Doctor Byam,
Said: 'Right oh, old fellow, we'll try 'em,
For I'm an adept, O,
At pumping in strepto
Since I was a surgeon in Siam.'

The patient, who hailed from New Zealing,
Said: 'Pray don't consider my feeling,
Provided you're certain
'Twill not go on hurtin',
I'll lie here and smile at the ceiling.'

These two very bloodthirsty men,
Injected five million, then ten,
But found that the strepto
Had suddenly crept to
Her feet—and the worst happened then!

Any day you may happen to meet
Her alone in the Hampstead High Street
In a box on four wheels
With a whistle that squeals;
And her hands do the job of her feet.

[In September 1919 K.M. went to San Remo, and, after a few weeks, took a little furnished cottage—the 'Casetta'–at Ospedaletti near by. I was with her in San Remo, but returned to England to my work as editor of *The Athenæum* as soon as she was settled into the 'Casetta' with L.M. For a time K.M. was very happy; but then illness and isolation and the everlasting sound of the sea began to depress her.]

Mrs. Nightingale: A Dream.

November. Walking up a dark hill with high iron fences at the sides of the road and immense trees over. I was looking for a midwife, Mrs. Nightingale. A little girl, barefoot, with a handkerchief over her head pattered up and put her chill hand in mine; she would lead me.

A light showed from a general shop. Inside a beautiful fair angry young woman directed me up the hill and to the right.

'You should have believed *me!*' said the child, and dug her nails into my palm.

There reared up a huge wall with a blank notice plastered on it. That was the house. In a low room, sitting by a table, a dirty yellow and black rug on her knees, an old hag sat. She had a grey handkerchief on her head. Beside her on the table was a jar of onions and a fork. I explained. She was to come to mother. Mother was very delicate: her eldest daughter was thirty-one and she had heart disease. 'So please come at once.'

'Has she any adhesions?' muttered the old hag, and she speared an onion, ate it and rubbed her nose.

'Oh, yes'—I put my hands on my breast—'many, many plural adhesions.'

'Ah, that's bad, that's very bad,' said the old crone, hunching up the rug so that through the fringe I saw her square slippers. 'But I can't come. I've a case at four o'clock.'

At that moment a healthy, bonny young woman came in with a bundle. She sat down by the midwife and explained, 'Jinnie has had hers already.' She un-wound the bundle too quickly: a new-born baby with round eyes fell forward on her lap. I felt the pleasure of the little girl beside me—a kind of quiver. The young woman blushed and lowered her voice. 'I got her to . . .' And she paused to find a very *medical private* word to describe washing. . . . 'To *navigate* with a bottle of English water,' she said, 'but it isn't all away yet.'

Mrs. Nightingale told me to go to the friend, Madame Léger, who lived on the terrace with a pink light before her house. I went. The terrace of houses was white and grey-blue in the moonlight with dark pines down the road. I saw the exquisite pink light. But just then there was a clanking sound behind me, and there was the little girl, bursting with breathlessness dragging in her arms a huge black bag. 'Mrs. Nightingale says you forgot this.'

So *I* was the midwife. I walked on thinking: 'I'll go and have a look at the poor little soul. But it won't be for a long time yet.'

Et in Arcadia Ego.

To sit in front of the little wood fire, your hands crossed in your lap and your eyes closed—to fancy you see again upon your eyelids all the dancing beauty of the day, to feel the flame on your throat as you used to imagine you felt the spot of yellow when Bogey held a buttercup under your chin . . . when breathing is such delight that you are almost afraid to breathe—as though a butterfly fanned its wings upon your breast. Still to taste the warm sunlight that melted in your mouth; still to smell the white waxy scent that lay upon the jonquil fields and the wild spicy scent of the rosemary growing in little tufts among the red rocks close to the brim of the sea. . . .

The moon is rising but the reluctant day lingers upon the sea and sky. The sea is dabbled with a pink the colour of unripe cherries, and in the sky there is a flying yellow light like the wings of canaries. Very stubborn and solid are the trunks of the palm trees. Springing from their tops the stiff green bouquets seem to cut into the evening air and among them, the blue gum trees, tall and slender with sickle-shaped leaves and drooping branches half blue, half violet. The moon is just over the mountain behind the village. The dogs know she is there; already they begin to howl and bark. The fishermen are shouting and whistling to one another as they bring in their boats, some young boys are singing in half-broken voices down by the shore, and there is a noise of children crying, little children with burnt cheeks and sand between their toes being carried to bed. . . .

I am tired, blissfully tired. Do you suppose that daisies feel blissfully tired when they shut for the night and the dews descend upon them?

Death.

December 17. When I had gone to bed I realized what it was that had caused me to 'give way'. It was the effort of being up, with a heart that won't work. Not my lungs at all. My despair simply disappeared—yes, simply. The weather was lovely. Every morning the sun came in and drew more squares of golden light on the wall, I looked round my bed on to a sky like silk. The day opened slowly, slowly like a flower, and it held the sun long, long before it slowly, slowly folded. Then my homesickness went. I not only didn't want to be in England, I began to love Italy, and the thought of it —the sun—even when it was too hot—always the sun— and a kind of *wholeness* which was good to bask in.

All these two years I have been obsessed by the fear of death. This grew and grew and grew gigantic, and this it was that made me cling so, I think. Ten days ago it went, I care no more. It leaves me perfectly cold. . . . Life either stays or goes.

I must put down here a dream. The first night I was in bed here, *i.e.* after my first day in bed, I went to sleep. And suddenly I felt my whole body *breaking up*. It broke up with a violent shock—an earthquake—and it broke like glass. A long terrible shiver, you understand— the spinal cord and the bones and every bit and particle quaking. It sounded in my ears a low, confused din, and there was a sense of floating greenish brilliance, like broken glass. When I woke I thought that there had been a violent earthquake. But all was still. It slowly dawned upon me—the conviction that in that dream I died. I shall go on living now—it may be for months, or for weeks or days or hours. Time is not. In that dream I died. The *spirit* that is the enemy of death and quakes so and is so tenacious was shaken out of me. I am

(December 15, 1919) a dead woman, and *I don't care.*
It might comfort others to know that one gives up
caring; but they'd not believe any more than I did until
it happened. And, oh, how strong was its hold upon
me! How I *adored* life and *dreaded* death!

I'd like to write my books and spend some happy
time with J. (not very much faith withal) and see L.
in a sunny place and pick violets—all kinds of flowers.
I'd like to do heaps of things, really. But I don't mind
if I do not do them. ... Honesty (why?) is the only
thing one seems to prize beyond life, love, death, everything. It alone remaineth. O you who come after me,
will you believe it? At the end *truth* is the only thing
worth having: it's more thrilling than love, more joyful
and more passionate. It simply can*not* fail. All else fails.
I, at any rate, give the remainder of my life to it and it
alone.

December 15. I'd like to write a *long, long* story on this
and call it 'Last Words to Life'. One *ought* to write it.
And another on the subject of HATE.

December. It often happens to me now that when I lie
down to sleep at night, instead of getting drowsy, I feel
more wakeful and, lying here in bed, I begin to *live*
over either scenes from real life or imaginary scenes.
It's not too much to say they are almost hallucinations:
they are marvellously vivid. I lie on my right side and
put my left hand up to my forehead as though I were

praying. This seems to induce the state. Then, for instance, it is 10.30 p.m. on a big liner in mid-ocean. People are beginning to leave the Ladies' Cabin. Father puts his head in and asks if 'one of you would care for a walk before you turn in. It's glorious up on deck.' That begins it. I am *there*. Details: Father rubbing his gloves, the cold air—the *night* air, the pattern of everything, the feel of the brass stair-rail and the rubber stairs. Then the deck—the pause while the cigar is lighted, the look of all in the moonlight, the *steadying* hum of the ship, the first officer on deck, so far aloft the bells, the steward going into the smoking-room with a tray, stepping over the high, brass-bound step. . . . All these things are far realer, more in detail, *richer* than life. And I believe I could go on until . . . There's *no end* to it.

I can do this about everything. Only there are no personalities. Neither am I there personally. People are only part of the silence, *not* of the pattern—vastly different from that part of the *scheme*. I could always do this to a certain extent; but it's only since I was really ill that this—shall we call it?—'consolation prize' has been given to me. My God! it's a marvellous thing.

I can call up certain persons—Doctor S. for instance. And then I remember how I used to say to J. and R. 'He was looking very beautiful to-day.' I did not know what I was saying. But when I so summon him and see him 'in relation', he *is* marvellously beautiful. There again he comes complete, to every detail, to the shape of his thumbs, to looking over his glasses, his lips as he writes, and particularly in all connected with putting the needle into the syringe. . . . I relive all this at will.

'Any children?' he said, taking his stethoscope as I struggled with my night-gown.

'No, no children.'

But what would he have said if I'd told him that until a few days ago I had a little child, aged five and three quarters, of indeterminate sex? Some days it was a boy. For two years now it had very often been a little girl. . . .

December. Surely I do know more than other people: I have suffered more, and endured more. I know how they long to be happy, and how precious is an atmosphere that is loving, a *climate* that is not frightening. Why do I not try to bear this in mind, and try to cultivate my garden? Now I descend to a strange place among strangers. Can I not make myself felt as a real personal force? (why should you?) Ah, but I *should.* I have had experiences unknown to them. I should by now have learnt C.'s obiter dictum—how true it might be. It *must* be.

[Towards the end of December, worried by the depression of her letters, I went to Ospedaletti for a fortnight to see K.M.]

December 30. Calm day. In garden read early poems in Oxford Book. Discussed our future library. In the evening read Dostoevsky. In the morning discussed the importance of 'eternal life'. Played our famous Stone Game (Cape Sixpence and Cornwall).[1]

December 31. Long talk over house. Foster said I could walk. Sea sounded like an island sea. Happy. Lovely fire in my bedroom. Succès éclatant avec demon before dinner. Listened to Wingley's fiddle. The wooden bed.

---

[1] The Stone Game was simple. You placed a largish stone at the extreme edge of a cliff, sat down about ten yards away and shied smaller stones at it. The one who first toppled it over received sixpence from the other. Hence the name, Cape Sixpence, which we gave to the cliff near Bandol where we first played the game.

JANUARY 1. J. PREPARES TO GO. DRYING FIGS ON the stove, and white socks drying from the mantelpiece. A dish of oranges and rain-wet leaves—a pack of cards on the table. It rains but it is warm. The jonquil is in bud. We linger at the door. L.M. sings.

January 2. J. left for London. The house very empty and quiet. I was ill all day—exhausted. In the afternoon fell asleep over my work and missed the post. My heart won't lie down. No post. During the night the cat picture became terrifying.

January 3. A load of wood. Sent review. Cold day. Miss S. called—deadly dull. Her yawn and recovery. Storm of wind and rain. I had nightmare about J. He and I 'separated'. Miss S. talked about tulips, but she makes all sound so fussy: the threads of her soul all ravelled.

January 4. Cold, wet, windy, terrible weather. Fought it all day. Horribly depressed. D. came to tea; but it was no good. Worked. Two wires from J. According to promise. I cannot write. The jonquils are out, weak and pale. Black clouds pull over.

Immediately the sun goes in I am overcome—again the black fit takes me. I *hate* the *sea*. There is naught to do but WORK. But how can I work when this awful weakness makes even the pen like a walking-stick?

January 5. Nuit blanche. Decided at 3 a.m. that D. was a homicidal maniac. *Certain* of this. Started my story, 'Late Spring'. A cold bitter day. Worked on Tchehov all day and then at my story till 11 p.m. Anna came. We talked about her to her face in English. No letters. Post Office strike. Anna's bow and velvet blouse.

January 6. Black day. Dark, no sky to be seen; a livid sea; a noise of boiling in the air. Dreamed the cats died of *anti-pneumonia*. Heart attack 8 a.m. Awful day. No relief for a moment. Couldn't work. At night changed the position of my bed. At five o'clock I thought I was at sea tossing—for ever. N.B.

January 7. On the veranda. I don't want a God to praise or to entreat, but to *share* my vision with. This afternoon looking at the primula after the rain. I want no one to dance and wave their arms. I only want to *feel* they see, too.

January 8. BLACK. A day spent in Hell. Unable to do anything. Took brandy. Determined not to weep—wept. Sense of isolation frightful. I shall die if I don't escape. Nauseated, faint, cold with misery. Oh, I *must* survive it somehow.

January 9. BLACK. Another of them. In the afternoon Foster came and agreed I must leave here. Somehow or other I wrote a column. Broke my watch glass. In the evening L.M. and I were more nearly friendly than we have been for years. I couldn't rest or sleep. The roaring of the sea was insufferable.

January 10. Spent the evening writing another column. Help me, God! And then L.M. came in to say I was half an hour slow. Just did it in time. Had talk with L.M. Our friendship is returning—in the old fashion. Thought out 'The Exile'.[1] Appalling night of misery.

January 11. Worked from 9.30 till a quarter after midnight only stopping to eat. Finished the story. Lay awake then until 5.30 too excited to sleep. In the sea drowned souls sang all night. I thought of everything in my life, and it all came back so vividly. . . . These are the worst days of my whole life.

January 12. Posted the story and a telegram. Very tired. The sea howled and boomed and roared away. When will this cup pass from me? Oh, misery! I cannot sleep. I lie retracing my steps—going over all the old life before. . . .

January 13. Bad day. A curious smoky effect over the coast. I crawled and crept about the garden in the afternoon. I feel terribly weak and all the time on the verge of breaking down. Tried to work; could not

[1] Afterwards called 'The Man without a Temperament'; see *Bliss*.

work. At six o'clock went back to bed. Had a dreadful nightmare.

January 14. Foster came: says my lung is remarkably better, but must rest absolutely for two months and not attempt to walk at all. I have got a 'bigger chance'. Bell rang at night. My eye pains me. *Cannot* get a move on. Dreamed about B. She gave me her baby to mind.

January 15. Sat in my room watching the day change to evening. The fire like a golden stag. *Thinking of the past* always; dreaming it over. The cotton plant has turned yellow. To-night the sea is *down*. P.O. strike. No, no letters.

January 16. Wrote and sent reviews. Stayed in bed, worked. Had a bath. The day was very lovely. I had to work hard. In the evening began my new story 'A Strange Mistake'.[1] P.O. strike for letters *and* telegrams. At night I could not sleep. My life in London seems immeasurably far and all like a dream. L.M. talked of herself as a child.

January 17. Postal strike: no letters, no wire. Tearing up and sorting the old letters. The feeling that comes— the anguish—the words that fly out into one's breast: My *darling!* My *wife!* Oh, what anguish! Oh, will it

[1] Subsequently called *The Wrong House:* see 'Something Childish, and Other Stories', where it is wrongly dated 1919.

ever be the same? Lay awake at night listening to the voices. Two men seemed to sing—a tenor and a baritone: then the drowned began.

January 18. No letters: strike still on. A fine day. But what is that to me? I am an *invalid*. I spend my life in bed. Read Shakespeare in the morning. I feel I cannot bear this silence to-day. I am *haunted* by thoughts.

January 19. No letters or papers. V. came; and Mrs. V. and Miss S. in white. 'The trouble I've had with you, Mrs. Murry, and the expense it's put me to—more fuss than if you'd died there.' The women against the flowers were so lovely—even Miss S. I had a dreadful crying fit about 'noise and cleanliness'. It was horrible.

January 20. Washed my hair. L.M. out all day. Here alone—a perfect day. I wandered in the garden. . . . There was a ship, white and solid on the water. Overcoat disappeared. The fire in my room and the double light. All was exquisitely beautiful. 'Good-bye.' It now believes we are going and it is safe.

January 21. A day like a dream. V.'s hair, stick, jacket, teeth, tie—all to be remembered. 'To use a *vulgarism*, I'm fed up.' The journey—the flowers—and these women here. Jinnie's black satin neckcloth and pearl pin. This exquisite cleanliness turns me into a cat.

[On this day K.M. finally left the Casetta for a nursing home in Mentone.]

January 22. Saw the doctor: a fool. The Casetta left to itself: the little winds blowing, the shutters shut, the cotton plant turning yellow. Spent a tiring morning. My heart hurts me. The meals downstairs are a fearful strain. But the people naïve.

January 23. Saw two of the doctors—an ass, and an ass. Spent the day at my window. It was very lovely and fair. But I was trying to work all day and could not get down to it. In the night had appalling nightmare.

January 24. Cousin C. brought the tiny dog to see me —a ravishing animal. The same despairing desire to work, and could not work. I suppose I started reviewing T. nine or ten times. Felt very tired as a result of this.

January 25. The meals here are a horror. I seem to be sitting hours and hours there, and the people are ugly. Nevertheless, thank God I *am* here, in sound of the train, in reach of the post.

January 26. Felt ill with fatigue and cold and my lungs hurt. It is because I am not working. All is a bit of a nightmare for that reason. My temper is so bad! I feel I am horrid and can't stop it. It's a bad feeling.

January 27. The woman who does the massage is not really any good. My life is queer here. I like my big airy room, but to *work* is so hard. At the back of my mind I am so wretched. But all the while I am thinking over my philosophy—the defeat of the personal.

January 28. I shall not remember what happened on this day. It is a blank. At the end of my life I may want it, may long to have it. There was a new moon: that I remember. But who came or what I did—all is lost. It's just a day missed, a day crossing the line.

January 30. I tried all day to work and feel *dog*-tired. Perhaps it's the massage. Jinnie came to see me and brought me a present from her little dog.

January 31. Changed my room for this other. I prefer it. It is more snug and there is only one bed.

February 1. My room is horrible. Very noisy: a constant clatter and a feeling as though it were *doorless*. French people don't care a hang how much noise they make. I hate them for it. Stayed in bed; felt very ill, but don't mind because of the reason. The food was really appalling: nothing to eat. At night *old Casetta* feelings, like madness. Voices and words and half-visions.

February 2. Connie and Jinnie came and brought a notice of my book ['Bliss']. I brought in more flowers.

Saw the lovely palm. Love will win if only I can stick to it. It will win after all and through all.

February 3. Went for a little walk in the garden and saw all the pale violets. The beauty of palm trees. I fell in love with a tree. Japonica is a lovely flower, but people never grow enough of it.

February 4. Horrible day. I lay all day and *half* slept in this new way—hearing voices.

February 5. Went for a drive. All the way gay. The house and the girl. Couldn't work: slept again. Dreadful pain in joints. Fearfully *noisy* house! Saw an orange tree, an exquisite shape against the sky: when the fruit is ripe the leaves are pale yellow.

February 6. Determined to review two books to-day and to get on with 'Second Helping'. Saw the *fool* of a doctor to-day. Diddle-dum-dum-dee! *Cod* is the only word! Bad-in-age! Flat-ter-ie! Gal-ant-ter-ie! Frogs!!! Vous pouvez vous promener. *Liar*. The palm tree. Did not finish review; but no matter, it goes.

February 7. House in a perfect uproar. Dreadfully nervous. Dressmaker came and her little apprentice who gave me the flowers. Had a bath—but all was in a tearing hurry and clatter. Had a strange dream. 'She is one with the moonlight.' George Sand—ma sœur.

February 8. To Villa Flora. In the garden with the unhappy woman lying on the hard bench. The Spanish brocade cloth—the piece of heliotrope. Jinnie's plan that I shall go and live there. Came back and wrote it all to J. in delight. I for the first time think I should like to join the Roman Catholic Church. I must have *something*.

[Shortly afterwards K.M. left the nursing home to stay at the Villa Flora with her cousin Miss Beauchamp and her friend Miss Fullerton, whose devoted care of her was rewarded by a rapid and remarkable improvement in her health.]

Anguish.

The postman was late. She rang and asked the eternal 'déjà passé?' and heard the eternal 'pas encore, Madame'. At last Armand appeared with a letter and the papers. The letter she read. And then it happened *again*, again there seemed to be a dreadful loud shaking and trembling: her heart leaped. She sank down in the bed. She began to weep and could not stop.

The first bell rang. She got up, she began to dress, crying and cold. The second bell. She sat down and steeled herself; her throat ached, ached. She powdered herself thickly and went downstairs. In the lift: 'Armand, cherchez-moi une voiture pour deux heures juste.' And then one hour and a quarter in the brilliant glaring noisy *salle*, sipping wine to stop crying, and seeing all the animals crack up the food. The waiters kept jerking her chair, offering food. It was no good.

She left and went upstairs, but that was fatal. Had she a home? A little cat? Was she any man's *wife?* Was it all over?

She dressed and went downstairs into the horrible hall, because there, with the *monde* drinking coffee, she dared not cry. A little brougham drove up with an old dragging man. She got in. 'A la poste!' Oh, these little broughams, what she had gone through in them! the blue-buttoned interior, the blue cords and ivory tassels, all, all! She leaned back and lifted her veil and dried her tears. But it was no use. The post office was full. She had to wait in a queue for the telegrams among horrible men who shouted over her shoulder, horrible men. And now, where? A dose of sal volatile at the chemist's. While he made it up she walked quickly up and down the shop, twisting her hands. There was a box of Kolynos. It spoke of him, him in her room, talking about the foam, saying he'd leave his behind. Four francs seventy-five.

She bought and drank the mixture, and now, where? She got into the cab—the old man hung at the door— she couldn't speak. Suddenly down the road on the opposite side, looking very grave came Frances. She crossed over and taking her hand said 'Deo gratias'. And she was silent a moment. Then she said suddenly, 'Come along and see M'Laren now. Let's fix it now this moment.' They waited in a very quiet room, rich with books and old dark coloured prints, and dark highly polished furniture. Frances went out for a preparatory talk and then came back for her and they entered the doctor's room. He was short, dry, with a clipped beard and fine brown eyes. A fire burned: there were books everywhere. German books too. Frances stayed while the long familiar careful examination went on again. The doctor took infinite pains. When he had done she dressed, and Frances said: 'Doctor, it's the desire of my life to cure this—little friend of mine. You must let me have her, you must let me do it.' And after a pause which the other thought final, he said: 'I think it would be ideal for her to be with you. She ought not to have to suffer noise and the constant sight of repellent people. She is highly sensitive and her disease—of such long standing, has increased it a thousandfold.' He was quiet, grave, gentle. Oh, if they could have known or seen her heart that had been stabbed and stabbed. But she managed to smile and thank the doctor, and then Frances put her back into the brougham, and it was arranged she would leave in a week.

All the afternoon she had been seeing wall-flowers. Let her never have a sprig of wall-flowers—if ever she had a garden. Oh, anguish of life! Oh, bitter, bitter Life! That reminded her of wall-flowers and Shakespeare. Yes, how in a *Winter's Tale*, Perdita refused gillyflowers in her garden. 'They call them nature's bastards.' She came back into her room and lay down. It was like Bavaria again, but worse, worse—and now she could not take a drug, or anything. She must just *bear it and go on.*

The Glimpse.

And yet one has these 'glimpses', before which all that one ever has written (what has one written?)—all (yes, all) that one ever has read, pales. . . . The waves, as I drove home this afternoon, and the high foam, how it was suspended in the air before it fell. . . . What is it that happens in that moment of suspension? It is timeless. In that moment (what *do* I mean?) the whole life of the soul is contained. One is flung up—out of life—one is 'held', and then,—down, bright, broken, glittering on to the rocks, tossed back, part of the ebb and flow.

I don't want to be sentimental. But while one hangs, suspended in the air, held—while I watched the spray, I was conscious *for life* of the white sky with a web of torn grey over it; of the slipping, sliding, slithering sea; of the dark woods blotted against the cape; of the flowers on the tree I was passing; and more—of a huge cavern where my selves (who were like ancient sea-weed gatherers) mumbled, indifferent and intimate . . . and this other self apart in the carriage, grasping the cold knob of her umbrella, thinking of a ship, of ropes stiffened with white paint and the wet, flapping oil-skins of sailors. . . . Shall one ever be at peace with oneself? Ever quiet and uninterrupted—without pain —with the one whom one loves under the same roof? Is it too much to ask?

February 29. Oh, to be a *writer*, a real writer given up

to it and to it alone! Oh, I failed to-day; I turned back, looked over my shoulder, and immediately it happened, I felt as though I too were struck down. The day turned cold and dark on the instant. It seemed to belong to summer twilight in London, to the clang of the gates as they close the garden, to the deep light painting the high houses, to the smell of leaves and dust, to the lamp-light, to that stirring of the senses, to the languor of twilight, the breath of it on one's cheek, to all those things which (I feel to-day) are gone from me for ever. . . . I feel to-day that I shall die soon and suddenly: but not of my lungs.

There are moments when Dickens is possessed by this power of writing: he is carried away. That is bliss. It certainly is not shared by writers to-day. The death of Cheedle: dawn falling upon the edge of night. One realizes exactly the mood of the writer and how he wrote, as it were, for himself, but it was not his will. He *was* the falling dawn, and he *was* the physician going to Bar. And again when . . .

> Le temps des lilas et le temps des roses
> Ne reviendra plus ce printemps-ci,
> Le temps des lilas et le temps des roses
> Est passé—le temps des œillets aussi.
>
> Le vent a changé—les cieux sont moroses
> Et nous n'irons pas couper et cueillir
> Les lilas en fleurs et les belles roses;
> Le printemps est triste et ne peut fleurir.

O joyeux et doux printemps de l'année
Qui vint, l'an passé, nous ensoleiller;
Notre fleur d'amour est si bien fânée
Las! que ton baiser ne peut l'éveiller.

Et toi, que fais-tu? pas de fleurs écloses
Point de gai soleil ni d'ombrages frais;
Le temps des lilas et le temps des roses
Avec notre amour est mort à jamais.

Life's a queer thing. I read this to-day, and in my mind I heard it sung in a very pure voice to a piano, and it seemed to me to be part of the great pain of youthful love.

Wickedness.

I kissed her. Her cheek felt cold, white, and somehow moist. It was like kissing a church candle. I looked into her eyes: they were pale, flickering with dim, far-off lights. She smelled faintly of incense. Her skirt was rubbed and bulged at the knees.

'But how could you say that about the Blessed Virgin!' said she. 'It must have hurt Our Lady so terribly.'

And I saw the B.V. throwing away her copy of *Je ne parle pas Français* and saying: 'Really, this K.M. is all that her friends say of her to me.'

Roosters and Hens.

By night and at early morning I love to listen to my darling roosters crowing to one another from lonely yards.

Each one has a different note: I have never heard two roosters crow alike. But the hens who seem from their cackle to be laying eggs all day long sound as like one another as ... as ... In fact there's no possible distinguishing between them. L.M. says they are not *all* laying eggs. Some of them are frightened, surprised, excited, or just—playful. But this seems to me to make the affair even *more* ... humiliating.

April 4. Easter eggs in the folded napkins. A Happy Easter. We drink to absent friends, but carelessly, not knowing whether to bow or no.

April 9. Cold and windy. Out of the window the writhing palms—the dust—the woman with a black veil. I feel I must live alone, alone, alone—with *artists* only to touch the door. Every artist cuts off his ear and nails it on the outside of the door for the others to shout into.

April 11. I never can remember what happens. It is so without outline. 'Yesterday' falls into the general shade. But all the time one looks back and there are wonders. There is always Miss H. stretching out her hands to the great defiant mosquito—crying with a kind of groan—'Oh, the *darlings!*' That remains for ever. And then one must never forget the dog which gets all the love of children. 'Going nice ta-tas, my ducksie pet!'

April 12. Went to the fish museum at Monaco. Must remember the bubbles as the man plunged the rod into the tanks. The young girl. How naice! Young girls make me feel forty. Well, one certainly doesn't want to look 21. The woman with her three little children at Monte. . . .

[At the end of April K.M. returned to England, to her house in Hampstead.]

August 9. 'And if a man will consider life in its whole circuit, and see how superabundantly it is furnished with what is extra-ordinary and beautiful and great, he shall soon know for what we were born.'

August 9. I should like to have a secret code to put on record what I feel to-day. If I forget it, may my right hand forget its cunning . . . the lifted curtain . . . the hand at the fire with the ring and stretched fingers . . . no, it's snowing . . . the telegram to say he's not . . . just the words *arrive* 8.31. But if I say more I'll give myself away.

[Later.] I wrote this because there is a real danger of forgetting *that kind* of intensity, and it won't do.

December 8, 1920. No, there is *no* danger of forgetting.

August 12. More beautiful by far than a morning in spring or summer. The mist—the trees standing in it—not a leaf moves—not a breath stirs. There is a faint smell of burning. The sun comes slowly—slowly the room grows lighter. Suddenly, on the carpet, there is a square of pale, red light. The bird in the garden goes 'snip—snip—snip'—a little wheezy, like the sound of a knife-grinder. The nasturtiums blaze in the garden: their leaves are pale. On the lawn, his paws tucked under him, sits the black and white cat. . . .

August. I cough and cough, and at each breath a dragging, boiling, bubbling sound is heard. I feel that my whole chest is boiling. I sip water, spit, sip, spit. I feel I must break my heart. And I can't expand my chest; it's as though the chest had collapsed. . . . Life is—getting a new breath. Nothing else counts.

'Can't you help me? Can't you?' But even while she asked him she smiled as if it didn't matter so much whether he could or couldn't.

My nature . . . my nerves . . . the question is whether I shall change or not. Per-sonally. . . . You see him? And he has a friend, a confidant, an old schoolfellow, small, shabby, with a wooden leg, whom he has rediscovered. He's married. The friend enters the new ménage. Little by little he gets to know the wife. No *tragedy.* He feels like a one-legged sparrow. Talking together in the house before she comes in. 'Is that you, Beaty? Can we have some tea?'

Let the sparrow—let the sparrow—suffer the sparrow to . . .

Charades. Roger of course commits suicide, cuts his throat with a paper knife and gurgles his life away.

[The following notes evidently refer to the first conception of the unfinished story called *Weak Heart*, which is included in 'The Doves' Nest' (see page 183). The date shows that K.M. had cherished the idea of the story a long while.]

September. The daughter of the watch-smith. Her piano-playing. Her weak heart, queer face, queer voice, *awful clothes.* The violets in their garden. Her little mother and father. The scene at the Baths: the coldness, the blueness of the children, her size in the red twill bathing-dress, trimmed with white braid. The steps down to the water—the rope across.

Edie has a brother Siegfried. 17. You never know whether he has begun to shave or not. He and Edie walk in arm in arm. . . . Her Sunday hat is *trimmed beyond words.*

Oh, that tree at the corner of May Street! I forgot it until this moment. It was dark and hung over the street like a great shadow. The father was fair and youthful to look at. He was a clock-maker.

[The following entries belong to September 1920, and were made on the journey to the Villa Isola Bella at Mentone, where K.M. spent the winter of that year.]

Feminine Psychology.

'It is said that the turtle-dove never drinks clear water, but always muddies it first with its foot so that it may the better suit its pensive mind.'

Isola Bella: How shall I buy it?

Southward Bound.

Lying facing the window I woke early. The blind was half pulled down. A deep pink light flew in the sky, and the shapes of the trees, ancient barns, towers, walls were all black. The pools and rivers were quicksilver. Nearing Avignon, the orchard in the first rays of sunlight shone with gold fruit: apples flashed like stars.

L.M.'s legs dangled. She dropped down, slowly waving her big grey legs, as though something pulled her, dragged her—the tangle of rich blue weeds on the red carpet.

'A-vig . . . Avig . . . Avig-non,' she said.

'One of the loveliest names in the world done to death,' said I. 'A name that spans the ancient town like a bridge.'

She was very impressed. But then George Moore *could* impress her.

Woman and Woman.

What I feel is: She is never for one fraction of a second unconscious. If I sigh, I know that her head lifts. I know that those grave large eyes solemnly fix on me: Why did she sigh? If I turn she suggests a cushion or another rug. If I turn again, then it is my back. Might she try to rub it for me? There is no escape. All night: a faint rustle, the smallest cough,

and her soft voice asks: 'Did you speak? Can I do anything?' If I do absolutely nothing then she discovers
my fatigue under my eyes. There is something profound and terrible in this eternal desire to establish
contact.

Man and Woman.

Mysterious is man and woman. She sat on a flat seat
in the corridor and he stood above her while the dark
fat man beat them up a couple of beds. She looked
sulky, stubborn and bored. But it was plain to see she
suited him.

'Bang on the door when you're ready, old girl!'

And the door slammed. He sat on the flap-seat,
smoothed his thin smooth hair, folded his bony hands.
A neat foot dangled from a trim ankle. The light shone
on his glasses. Seeing him thus one could not imagine
a man who looked less like a woman's man. But I
admired him immensely. I was proud of them as
'made in England'.

Breakfast Time.

It grew hot. Everywhere the light quivered green-
gold. The white soft road unrolled, with plane trees
casting a trembling shade. There were piles of pump-
kins and gourds: outside the house the tomatoes were
spread in the sun. Blue flowers and red flowers and
tufts of deep purple flared in the road-side hedges. A
young boy, carrying a branch, stumbled across a

yellow field, followed by a brown high-stepping little goat. We bought figs for breakfast, immense thin-skinned ones. They broke in one's fingers and tasted of wine and honey. Why is the northern fig such a chaste fair-haired virgin, such a *soprano?* The melting contraltos sing through the ages.

England and France.

The great difference: England so rich, with the green bowers of the hops and gay women and children with their arms lifted, pausing to watch the train. A flock of yellow hens, led by a red rooster, streamed across the edge of the field. But France: an old man in a white blouse was cutting a field of small clover with an old-fashioned half-wooden scythe. The tops of the flowers were burnt; the stooks (are they stooks?) were like small heaps of half-burned tobacco.

[Marie of the following notes was the *bonne* at the Villa Isola Bella.]

Marie.

October. She is little and grey with periwinkle—I feel inclined to write peritwinkle—blue eyes and swift, sweeping gestures. Annette said she is 'une personne très supérieure—la veuve d'un cocher,' and 'qu'elle a son appartement à Nice.... Mais, que voulez-vous? La vie est si chère. On est forcé.' But Marie does not look like any of these imposing, substantial things. She is far too gay, too laughing, too light, to have ever

been more than a feather in the coachman's hat. As
to an *appartement*, I suspect it was a chair at a window
which overlooked a market.

Throttling, strangling by the throat, a helpless,
exhausted little black silk bag.

But one says not a word and to the best of one's
belief gives no sign. I went out into the gentle rain
and saw the rainbow. It deepens; it shone down into
the sea and it faded: it was gone. The small gentle
rain fell on the other side of the world. Frail—Frail.
I felt Life was no more than this.

Marie and the Cauliflower.

'*Mon pauvre mari* rolled over and said: *Tu as peur?
Que tu es bête! Ce sont des rats. Douze encore.*' I thought,
after she told me, and these words kept rippling and
rippling through my mind, something had disturbed
the long silent forgotten surface. How many of his
words were remembered? Did anybody ever quote
the living words he'd spoken? '*Tu as peur? Que tu es
bête!*' Words spoken at night, in the dark, strangely
intimate, reassuring. He turned over and lifted himself in his grave as Marie spoke. Mournful, mournful. . . .

'What about a cauliflower?' I said. 'A cauliflower
with white sauce.'

'But they are so dear, Madame,' wailed Marie. 'So
dear. One little cauliflower for 2 fr. 50. It's robbery,
it's . . .'

Suddenly through the kitchen window I saw the moon. It was so marvellously beautiful that I walked out of the kitchen door, through the garden and leaned over the gate before I knew what I was doing. The cold bars of the gate stopped me. The moon was full, transparent, glittering. It hung over the sighing sea. I looked at it for a long time. Then I turned round, and the little house faced me—a little white house quivering with light, a house like a candle shining behind a feather of mimosa-tree. I had utterly forgotten these things when I was ordering the dinner. I went back to the kitchen.

'Let us have a cauliflower at any price,' I said firmly.

And Marie muttered, bending over a pot—*could* she have understood?—'*En effet*, the times are dangerous!'

Foundlings.

'Does nobody want that piece of bread and butter?' says L.M. You would really think from her tone that she was saving the poor little darling from the river or worse, willing to adopt it as her own child and bring it up so that it never should know it was once unwanted. She cannot bear to see solitary little pieces of bread and butter or lonely little cakes—or even a lump of sugar that someone has cruelly, heartlessly left in his saucer. And when you offer her the big cake, she says resignedly: 'Oh, well, my dear, I'll just try', as though she knew how sensitive and easily hurt the

poor old chap's feelings were, if he's passed by. After
all, it can't hurt her.

L.M. is also exceedingly fond of bananas. But she
eats them so slowly, so terribly slowly. Ah, they know
it—somehow they realize what is in store for them
when she reaches out her hand. I have seen bananas
turn absolutely livid with terror, or grow pale—pale
as ashes.

The Kiss.

. . . I kissed her. Her flesh felt cold, pale, soft. I
thought of nuns who have prayed all night in cold
churches. . . . All her warmth and colour and passion
she had offered up in prayer, in cold ancient churches.
. . . She was chill, severe, pale; the light flickered in
her raised eyes like the light of candles; her skirt was
worn shiny over her peaked knees; she smelled faintly
of incense. 'No, Father. Yes, Father. Do you think so,
Father?' (But still I haven't said what I wanted to
say.) October 18, 1920.

The Doll.

'Well, look!' muttered Miss Sparrow.[1] 'I've nothing
to be ashamed of. Look as much as you like. I defy you.
It's what I've wanted all my life,' she cried brokenly,
'and now I've got it. I defy you. I defy the world!'
And she drew herself up in front of the window,
proudly, proudly; her eyes flashed, her lips gleamed.

[1] See entry of January 24, 1922.

She pressed the doll to her flat bosom. She was the Unmarried Mother.

Of course, I *can't* write that. I'm surprised to have made such a crude note. That's the raw idea, as they say. What I ought to do, though, is to write it, *somehow*, immediately, even if it's not good enough to print. My chief fault, my overwhelming fault is *not writing* it out. Well, now that I know it (and the disease is of very long standing), why don't I begin, at least, to follow a definite treatment? It is my experience that when an 'evil' is recognized, *any* delay in attempting to eradicate it is fatally weakening. And I, who love order, with my mania for the 'clean sweep', for every single thing being ship-shape—I to know there's such an ugly spot in my mind! Weeds flourish in neglect. I must keep my garden open to the light and in order. I must at all costs plant these bulbs and not leave them (oh, shameful!) to rot on the garden paths. To-day (October 18, 1920) is Monday. I have raised my right hand and sworn. Am I ever happy except when overcoming difficulties? Never. Am I ever free from the sense of guilt, even? Never. After I had finished that slight sketch, *The Young Girl*, wasn't there a moment which surpasses all other moments? Oh, yes. Then—why do you hesitate? How can you? I take my oath. Not one day shall pass without I write something—original.

December 14. The baby became covered with inkspots and served as a little reminder for days of the things she had forgotten to say and the things she might have said so differently.

The Little Cat.

'Here he used to sit and sometimes on the path below there sat a small white and yellow cat with a tiny flattened face. It sat very still and its little peaked shadow lay beside it. . . .

'This little cat never ran straight. It wound its way along the path, skirting the tufts of grass, crept now by the fence, now to the side of a rubbish-heap, and its little paws seemed to touch the ground as lightly as possible as though it were afraid of being followed —traced.'

I shan't say it like that. It's only a note. But Ah, my darling, how often have I watched your small, silent progress! I shall not forget you, my little cat, as you ran along your beat on this whirling earth.

When Jean-Paul was undressed, his breast was like a small cage of bent bamboos. And she hated to see it. 'Cover yourself!' And he shot his small arms into his woollen shirt.

Why Suffer?

'I don't want you to be other than yourself. . . .'

'But if I am myself I won't do what you ask me to do. . . . I feel its forcing me. It's not me; it's not my *geste*.'

They looked at each other and for some reason they smiled, actually *smiled*.

'I really and truly don't *know* what I want to do. Life isn't so simple as all that, you know. . . .'

And the music went on, gay, soothing, reassuring. All will be well, said the music. Life is so easy . . . so easy. Why suffer . . .?

This is the music when the elephants come in to drink out of bottles. Then the clown comes in and takes the bottles away and drinks himself.

The Last Waiting-Room.

One must write a story about a doctor's waiting-room. The glass doors with the sun from outside shining through; the autumn trees pale and fine; the cyclamen, like wax. Now a cart shakes by.

Think of the strange places that illness carries one into; the strange people among whom one passes from hand to hand; the succession of black-coated gentlemen to whom she'd whispered 99, 44, 1—2—3. The last waiting-room. All before had been so cheerful.

'Then you don't think my case is hopeless?'

'The disease is of long standing, but certainly *not* hopeless.' This one, however, leaned back and said: 'You really want to know?'

'Yes, of course. Oh, you can be quite frank with me.'

'Then, I DO!'

The carriage came and drove her away, her head buried in her collar.

But the champagne was no good at all. I had to drink it because it was there; but there was something positively malicious in the way the little bubbles hurled themselves to the brim, danced, broke. They seemed to be jeering at me.

Suffering.

I should like this to be accepted as my confession.

There is no limit to human suffering. When one thinks: 'Now I have touched the bottom of the sea— now I can go no deeper,' one goes deeper. And so it is for ever. I thought last year in Italy, Any shadow more would be death. But this year has been so much more terrible that I think with affection of the Casetta! Suffering is boundless, it is eternity. One pang is eternal torment. Physical suffering is—child's play. To have one's breast crushed by a great stone—one could laugh!

I do not want to die without leaving a record of my belief that suffering can be overcome. For I do believe it. What must one do? There is no question of what is called 'passing beyond it'. This is false.

One must *submit*. Do not resist. Take it. Be over-whelmed. Accept it fully. Make it *part of life*.

Everything in life that we really accept undergoes a change. So suffering must become Love. This is the mystery. This is what I must do. I must pass from personal love to greater love. I must give to the whole of life what I gave to one. The present agony will pass—if it doesn't kill. It won't last. Now I am like a man who has had his heart torn out—but—bear it— bear it! As in the physical world, so in the spiritual world, pain does not last for ever. It is only so terribly acute now. It is as though a ghastly accident had happened. If I can cease reliving all the shock and horror of it, cease going over it, I will get stronger.

Here, for a strange reason, rises the figure of Doctor Sorapure. He was a good man. He helped me not only to bear pain, but he suggested that perhaps bodily ill-health is necessary, is a repairing process, and he was always telling me to consider how man plays but a part in the history of the world. My simple kindly doctor was pure of heart as Tchehov was pure of heart. But for these ills one is one's own doctor. If 'suffering' is not a repairing process, I will make it so. I will learn the lesson it teaches. These are not idle words. These are not the consolations of the sick.

Life is a mystery. The fearful pain will fade. I must turn to work. I must put my agony into something, change it. 'Sorrow shall be changed into joy.'

It is to lose oneself more utterly, to love more deeply, to feel oneself part of life—not separate.

Oh Life! accept me—make me worthy—teach me.

I write that. I look up. The leaves move in the garden, the sky is pale, and I catch myself weeping. It is hard—it is hard to make a good death. . . .

To live—to live—that is all. And to leave life on this earth as Tchehov left it and Tolstoi.

After a dreadful operation I remember that when I thought of the pain of being stretched out, I used to cry. Every time I felt it again, and it was unbearable.

That is what one must control. Queer! The two people left are Tchehov—dead—and unheeding, indifferent Doctor Sorapure. They are the two good men I have known.

19-12-1920.   KATHERINE MANSFIELD.

At the Bay.

At last the milk-white harbour catches the glitter and the gulls floating on the trembling water gleam like the shadows within a pearl.

[See *Six Years After*, 'The Doves' Nest', p. 115.)

The house dog comes out of his kennel dragging the heavy chain and kalop-kalops at the water standing cold in the iron pan. The house cat emerges from nowhere and bounds on to the kitchen window sill waiting for her spill of warm morning milk.

[See *At the Bay*, 'The Garden Party', p. 10.]

Morning Children.

Children! Children!

Oh no. Not yet. Oh, it can't be time. Go away. I won't. Oh, why must I?

Children! Children!

They are being called by the cold servant girls.

But they simply can't get up. They simply must have one more little sleep—the best sleep of all—the warm, soft, darling little rabbit of a sleep.... Just let me hug it one minute more before it bounds away.

Soft little girls rolled up in rounds, just their bunch of curls showing over the sheet top; little long pale boys stretching out their slender feet; other little boys lying on their bellies pressing their heads into the pillow; tiny little fellows with fresh-cut hair sprouting from a tuft; little girls on their backs, their fists clenched, the bed-clothes anyhow, one foot dangling; girls with pig-tails or rings of white paper snails instead of hair.... And now there is the sound of plunging water and all those youthful, warm bodies, the tender exposed boy children, and the firm compact little girls, lie down in the bath tubs and ruffle their shoulders scattering the bright drops as birds love to do with their wings....

Squeech! Squeech! Tchee! Quee! Little boys with plastered hair, clean collars and brand new boots squeak from the nursery to the lobby to the cupboard under the stairs where the school kits are hung. Furious young voices cry: 'Who's *stolen* my ink-eraser that was in the well of my pencil box?'

They hiss through their teeth at the stolid servant girls carrying the porridge pots: 'You've been at this! Thief! Spy!!'

The Stranger.

'You merely find yourself in the old position of trying to change me. And I refuse to be changed. I won't change. If I don't feel these things—I don't feel them and there's an end of it.'

For a moment he stood there, cold, frigid, grasping the door-handle, staring not at her but over her head. He looked like a stranger who had opened her door by accident, and felt it necessary, for some reason or other, to explain the accident before he closed it again and went out of her life for ever.

Weak Tea.

. . . 'I have just partaken of that saddest of things—a cup of *weak* tea. Oh, why must it be weak! How much more than pathetic it is to hear someone say as she puts it down before you: 'I am afraid it is rather weak.' One feels such a brute to take advantage of it until it is a little stronger. I grasp the cup; it seems to quiver— to breathe—'coward!' I confess, I can never hear a person at a tea-party say (in that timid whisper you know, as though they were shamefully conscious): '*Very* weak for me, please,' without wanting to burst into tears. Not that I like desperately strong tea—No, let it be a moderate strength—tea that rings the bell. Very strong tea does seem to give you your penny back—in the tea-pot from the taste of it.

Now and again Fred talked in his sleep. But even then you could say he was quiet. . . . She would wake up and hear him say suddenly: 'it wants a couple of screws,' or 'try the other blade,' but never more than that.

The Change.

For a long time she said she did not want to change anything in him, and she meant it. Yet she hated things in him and wished they were otherwise. Then she said she did not want to change anything in him and she meant it. And the dark things that she had hated she now regarded with indifference. Then she said she did not want to change anything in him. But now she loved him so that even the dark things she loved, too. She wished them there; she was not indifferent. Still they were dark and strange but she loved them. And it was for this they had been waiting. They changed. They shed their darkness—the curse was lifted and they shone forth as Royal Princes once more, as creatures of light.

The Rivers of China.

She sat on the end of the box ottoman buttoning her boots. Her short fine springy hair stood out round her head. She wore a little linen camisole and a pair of short frilled knickers.

'Curse these buttons,' she said, tugging at them. And then suddenly she sat up and dug the handle of the button hook into the box ottoman.

'Oh dear,' she said, 'I do wish I hadn't married. I wish I'd been an explorer.' And then she said dreamily, 'The Rivers of China, for instance.'

'But what do you know about the rivers of China,

darling,' I said. For Mother knew no geography whatever; she knew less than a child of ten.

'Nothing,' she agreed. 'But I can *feel* the kind of hat
I should wear.' She was silent a moment. Then she
said, 'If Father hadn't died I should have travelled
and then ten to one I shouldn't have married.' And
she looked at me dreamily—looked through me, rather.

Snow-Mountains.

Have you noticed how very *smug* those mountains
look that are covered with snow all the year round.
They seem to expect me to be so full of admiring awe.
It never seems to enter their silly tops to wonder
whether it isn't rather dull to be so for ever and ever
above suspicion.

Cultivated Minds.

Such a cultivated mind doesn't really attract me.
I admire it, I appreciate all 'les soins et les peines' that
have gone to produce it—but it leaves me cold. After
all, the adventure is over. There is now nothing to do
but to trim and to lop and to keep back—all faintly
depressing labours. No, no, the mind I love must still
have wild places, a tangled orchard where dark dam-
sons drop in the heavy grass, an overgrown little wood,
the chance of a snake or two (real snakes), a pool that
nobody's fathomed the depth of—and paths threaded
with those little flowers planted by the mind. It must
also have *real* hiding-places, not artificial ones—not

gazebos and mazes. And I have never yet met the cultivated mind that has not had its shrubbery. I loathe and detest shrubberies.

Let me remember when I write about that fiddle how it runs up lightly and swings down sorrowful; how it *searches*—

In the white lace, the spreading veil and the pearls she looked like a gull. But a quick hungry gull with an absolutely insatiable appetite for bread. 'Come feed me! Feed me!' said that quick glare. It was as though all her vitality, her cries, her movements, her wheelings depended upon the person on the bridge who carried the loaf.

The Voyage of 'The Bugle'.

No, no, said Miss P., that really isn't fair. I love serious books. Why, I don't know when I've enjoyed a book as much as—as—Dear me! How silly! It's on the tip of my tongue—Darwin's . . . one moment—it's coming—Darwin's Decline and Fall. . . . No, no, that wasn't the one. That's not right now. Tchuh! Tchuh! you know how it is—I can see it quite plainly and yet . . . I've got it! Darwin's Descent of Man! . . . Was that the one—though? Do you know *now* I'm not certain? I feel it was, and yet it's unfamiliar. This is most extraordinary. And yet I enjoyed it so much.

There was a ship. Ah! *that's* brought it back. Of course, of course! *That* was the one. Darwin's Voyage of the Bugle!

'La mère de Lao-Tse a conçu son fils rien qu'en regardant filer une étoile.'

December 27. When I stuck the small drawing to the side of the mirror frame I realized that the seal—the mark—the *cachet rouge*—had been set on the room. It had then become the room of those two, and not her room any more. It is not that the room was dead before, but how it has gained in life! Whence has come the tiny bouquet of tangerine fruits, the paste-pot on the writing-table, the fowl's feather stuck in Ribni's hair,[1] the horn spectacles on the Chinese embroidery. The 'order' in which I live is not changed, but enriched; in some strange way it is enlarged.

This is *en effet* just the effect of his mind upon mine. Mysterious fitness of our relationship! And all those things which he does impose on my mind please me so deeply that they seem to be *natural* to me. It is all part of this feeling that he and I, different beyond the dream of difference, are yet an *organic whole*. We are, as I said yesterday, the two sides of the medal, separate, distinct and yet making one. I do not feel that I need another to fulfil my being, and yet having him, I

[1] 'Ribni' was a Japanese doll belonging to K.M., so named after 'Captain Ribnikow', the Japanese spy who is the hero of Kuprin's remarkable story of that title.

possess something that without him I would lack. In fact we are—apart from everything else—each other's *critic* in that he 'sees' me, I see myself reflected as more than I appear and yet not more than I AM, and so I believe it is with him. So, to be together is apart from all else *an act of faith in ourselves.*

I went out into the garden just now. It is starry and mild. The leaves of the palm are like down-drooping feathers; the grass looks soft, unreal, like moss. The sea sounded, and a little bell was ringing, and one fancied—was it real, was it imaginary?—one heard a body of sound, one heard all the preparations for night within the houses. Someone brings in food from the dark, lamp-stained yard. The evening meal is prepared. The charcoal is broken, the dishes are clattered; there is a soft movement on the stairs and in the passages and doorways. In dusky rooms where the shutters are closed the women, grave and quiet, turn down the beds and see that there is water in the water-jugs. Little children are sleeping. . . .

Does it always happen that while you look at the star you feel the other stars are dancing, flickering, changing places, almost playing a game on purpose to bewilder you? It is strange that there are times when I feel the stars are not at all *solemn:* they are secretly gay. I felt this to-night. I sat on the cane chair and leaned against the wall. I thought of him contained in the little house against which I leaned—within reach—within call. I remembered there was a time when this thought was a distraction. Oh, it might have been a sweet distraction—but there it was! It took away from my power to work. . . . I, as it were, made him my short story. But that belongs to the Past. . . . One has passed beyond it.

The Question.
January. Does one ever know? One never knows. She
realized how foolish it would be to ask the question:
'What are you thinking of?' And yet if she did not ask
the question she would never be certain that he was
not thinking of . . . Even if she asked, how could she
be certain he did not make up the answer.

[An unposted letter.]

Your letters sounded insincere to me; I did not
believe them. People *don't* write such things; they only
think they do, or they read them in books. But real
life is on quite another plane. If I were not ill, I still
would have withdrawn from the world because of my
hatred of insincerity. It makes me dreadfully uncomfortable and unhappy. I could have answered your
letter just in your vein and 'accepted' it, you knowing
how I accepted it and I knowing that you knew—but
it wouldn't have lasted. It would have been another
cul de sac relationship. What good would that have
been to either of us?

You see—to me—life and work are two things in-
divisible. It's only by being true to life that I can be
true to art. And to be true to life is to be *good, sincere,
simple, honest*. I think other people have given you a
wrong idea of me, perhaps. I like to love only my
friends. I have no time for anything less precious.
Friendship *is* an adventure; but do we agree about

the meaning of the word 'adventure'? That's so important! That's where I feel we would quarrel. If you came on to *our* boat should we have understood one another?

You must not think I am 'prejudiced' or unfair. I am not. I still wish it were possible; but I cannot, and I won't pretend. Let us really and truly know where we are first. Let us be open with each other and not concealing anything.

January 14. 'To be happy with you seems such an impossibility! It requires a luckier star than mine! It will never be. . . . The world is too brutal for me.' [Keats to Fanny Brawne, August 1820.]

[*February?*] Le travail, même mauvais, vaut mieux que la rêverie.

'But I can't see why you should mind, so much,' she said for the hundredth time. 'I can't see what it is you object to. It isn't as though people would notice you even. Goodness me! I'm always meeting them since . . . since . . .' She broke off. 'And it seems such a waste, too. There it is, standing in the hall, doing nothing. It seems so ungrateful, after it's been lent to you, not to give it a trial at least. Why don't you say something?'

She was pinning on her hat in front of the mirror in the sitting-room. Her outdoor jacket and gloves lay across a chair. And when he still didn't answer her she made a little weary hopeless face at the mirror which meant: 'Oh dear, we're in one of our moods again!'

'If it's *me* you're thinking of by any chance,' she said quickly, snatching at the jacket . . .

Here is Marie with the supper. And I shall have to endure her until it is over. But that is not important: what *is*, is that I have not written anything to-day worth a sou. I have passed the day in a kind of idleness. Why? Does it take so long to begin again? Is it my old weakness of will?

Oh, I must not yield! I must this evening, after my supper, get something done. It's not so terribly hard after all. And how shall I live my *good life* if I am content to pass even one day in idleness? It won't do. *Control*—of all kinds. How easy it is to lack control in little things! And once one does lack it the small bad habits—tiny perhaps—spring up like weeds and choke one's will. That is what I find.

My temper is bad; my personal habits are not above reproach; I'm ungracious—mentally untidy. I let things pass that I don't understand (unpardonable!) and I excuse myself, invent pretexts for not working. Yet is my desire to be idle greater than my desire to work? Is my love of *rêverie* greater than my love of action? Treacherous habit! Habit above all others evil and of long standing! I must give it up *at once* or lose my self-respect. . . . He that faileth in little things shall not succeed in great things. Even my handwriting. From this moment *it* too must change. After supper I must start my Journal and keep it day by day. But *can* I be honest? If I lie, it's no use.

[I joined K.M. at Mentone in February 1921, when *The Athenæum* ceased separate publication. At the beginning of May K.M. left Mentone for Switzerland, while I returned to England to lecture at Oxford, rejoining her at Sierre at the end of May. After a little while we went up to Montana to a furnished chalet ('Chalet des Sapins'). For some weeks the action of K.M.'s heart in the high altitude gave her great pain.]

May 5. Genève: Salle d'attente. The snow lay like silver light on the tops of the mountains.

In the chill, greenish light, the wide motionless rivers looked as though they were solid, and the pale furrowed earth, with white fruit-trees like coral branches, looked as if it were water.

Later. The station clock.

[An unposted letter.]

The *Tig Courier*, Sir, is a weekly paper that pays you £950 a year for an article, personal as possible, the more intimate the better.

For three days the Editor has been waiting for your copy. To-night she got a postcard written in a train; but that was all. Will you tell her

(*a*) your reasons for withholding it (as subtle as you like) or (*b*) when she may expect it.

Address: Tig, Stillin, Bedfordshire.

[An unposted letter.]

Dear B. I can't tell you how glad I am to hear you are dancing again—'albeit delicately', as you say.

> Lo! how sweetly the Graces do it foot
>   To the instrument!
> They daunzen deftly and singen sooth
>   In their merriement.

That means you are really better. Don't get ill again. Isn't it awful—being ill! I lie all day on my old balcony lapping up eggs and cream and butter with no one but a pet gold-finch to bear me tumpanēē. I must say the gold-finch is a great lamb. He's jet tame, and this morning after it had rained he came for his Huntley and Palmer crumb with a little twinkling rain-drop on his head. I never saw anyone look more silly and nice. Switzerland is full of birds, but they are mostly stodgy little German trots flown out of Appenrodt's catalogue. . . . But all Switzerland is on the side of the stodges. . . .

[An unposted letter.]

I keep walking and walking round this letter, treading on my toes and with my tail in the air; I don't know where to settle. There's so much to say and the day is so fine. Well, here goes, darling.

The journey to Geneva took no time. My watchet seemed to be racing the train. We arrived some time

after one, and I went and sat on a green velvet chair
while L.M. saw to things. I suppose we had a long
wait there; it did not seem long. Ever since early
morning those mountains that I remembered from last
time had been there—huge, glittering, with snow like
silver light on their tops. It was absolutely windless,
and though the air was cold, it was cold like spring. In
fact (perhaps you realize I am putting a terrific curb
on myself) it was delicious. Only to breathe was enough.
Then we got into an omnibus train, and it waddled
slowly round the lake, stopping at every tiny station.
Germans were in the carriage; in fact, I was embedded
in Germans, huge ones—*Vater und die Mama und
Hänse*. Every time we saw a lilac-bush, they all cried
Schön! This was very *old-world*. There was also a notice
in the carriage to say that the company had thought-
fully provided a *cabinet*. This they read aloud—first,
Vater, then die Mama and then little Hänse.

We arrived at Clarens just as the station clock
(which was a cuckoo clock: that seems to me awfully
touching, doesn't it to you?) struck seven, and a motor-
car, like a coffee-mill, flew round and round the fields
to Baugy. Oh dear, you realize I'm just telling you
facts. The *embroidery* I'll have to leave for now. The
hotel is simply admirable so far. Too clean. Spick is
not the word, nor is span. Even the sprays of white lilac
in my room were fresh from the laundry. I have two
rooms and a huge balcony. And so many mountains
that I haven't even begun to climb them yet. They

are superb. The views from the windows, Betsy, over fields, little mushroom-like chalets, lake, trees, and then mountains, are overwhelming. So is the green velvet and flesh-pink satin suite in the salon, with copper jugs for ornaments and a picture on the wall called *Jugendidylle*. More of this later.

I am posing here as a lady with a weak heart and lungs of Spanish leather. It seems to 'go down' for the present. Well, I had dinner in my room: consommé, fish with cream sauce, roast turkey, new potatoes, braised laitue, and two little tiny babas smothered in cream. I had to send the turkey and trimmings away. Even then . . .

Saint-Galmier is superseded by Montreux,[1] which the label says is saturated with carbonic acid gas. But my physiology book said this was deadly poison and we only breathed it out—never unless we were desperate, took it in. However, according to Doctors Ritter, Spingel, and Knechtli, it's marvellous for gravel and makes the water sparkil like champagne. These are the Minor Mysteries. . . .

June 8. For the first time since the war I talked German to a German. 'Wollen Sie fragen ob man warten kann?' And so on. It was simply extraordinary. Why?

July. Montana. One thing I am determined upon. And that is *to leave no sign.* There was a time—it is not so

[1] Saint-Galmier and Montreux are both mineral waters.

long ago—when I should have written *all* that has happened since I left France. But now I deliberately
choose to tell no living soul. I keep silence as Mother
kept silence. And though there are moments when the
old habit 'tempts' me and I may even get so far as to
write a page, they are only moments, and each day
they are easier to conquer.

Chalet des Sapins, Montana. Just as now I say scarcely
a word about my treacherous heart. If it's going to
stop, it is going to stop, and there's an end of it. But
I have been in this little house for nearly two days now,
and it has not *once* quietened down. What dread to
live in! But what's the use of saying aught? No, my
soul, be quiet. . . .

July 10. And now, just as I felt a little better and less
worried about my HEAD and my heart, the gland has
become inflamed and all the surrounding tissue, too.
It looks as though an abscess were forming. So here is
another *scare*. And with it, I've one of my queer
attacks when I feel nauseated all the time and can't
bear light or noise or heat or cold. Shall I get through
this, too? It is not easy still to find the courage to cope
with these onslaughts. . . .

July 13. Went to the Palace, and had the gland punc-
tured. It is very unlikely that they will save the skin.
I am sure, from the feeling, that they won't, and that
this affair is only beginning. I shall be back at the

Palace before the week is out. In the meantime I am exhausted and can't write a *stroke*.

Well, I must confess I have had an idle day. God knows why. All was to be written, but I just didn't write it. I thought I could, but I felt tired after tea and rested instead. Is it good or bad in me to behave so? I have a sense of guilt, but at the same time I know that to rest is the very best thing I can do. And for some reason there is a kind of booming in my head— which is horrid. But marks of earthly degradation still pursue me. I am not crystal clear. Above all else I do still lack application. It's not right. There is so much to do, and I do so little. Life would be almost perfect here if only when I was *pretending* to work I always was working. But that is surely not too hard. Look at the stories that wait and wait just at the threshold. Why don't I let them in? And their place would be taken by others who are lurking beyond just out there —waiting for the chance.

Next Day. Yet take this morning, for instance. I don't want to write anything. It's grey; it's heavy and dull. And short stories seem unreal and not worth doing. I don't want to write; I want to *live*. What does she mean by that? It's not easy to say. But there you are!

Queer, this habit of mine of being garrulous. And I don't mean that any eye but mine should read this.

This is—*really private*. And I must say—nothing affords me the same relief. What happens as a rule is, if I go on long enough, I *break through*. Yes, it's rather like tossing very large flat stones into the stream. The question is, though, how long this will prove efficacious. Up till now, I own, it never has failed me. . . .

One's sense of the importance of small events is very *juste* here. They are not important at all. . . .!? Strange! I suddenly found myself outside the library in Wöris-hofen: spring—lilac—*rain*—books in black bindings.

And yet I love this quiet clouded day. A bell sounds from afar; the birds sing one after another as if they called across the tree-tops. I love this settled stillness, and this feeling that, at any moment, down may come the rain. Where the sky is not grey, it is silvery white, streaked with little clouds. The only disagreeable feature of the day is the flies. They are really mad-dening, and there is nothing really to be done for them: I feel that about hardly anything.

The Barmaid.

She had an immense amount of fuzzy hair piled up on top of her head, and several very large rings, which from their bright flashing look, you felt certain were engagement-rings.

Above all cooking smells I hate that of mutton chops. It is somehow such an ill-bred smell. It reminds me of commercial travellers and second-class, N.Z.

I'll stand in front of the house and knock, and when

the door is opened, run in past the maid and call for whoever is there.

Should you say wasted? No, not really. Something is gathered. This quiet time brings one nearer.

July. I finished *Mr. and Mrs. Dove* yesterday. I am not altogether pleased with it. It's a little bit made up. It's not inevitable. I mean to imply that those two may not be happy together—that that is the kind of reason for which a young girl marries. But have I done so? I don't think so. Besides, it's not *strong* enough. I want to be nearer—far, far nearer than that. I want to use all my force even when I am taking a fine line. And I have a sneaking notion that I have, at the end, used the Doves *unwarrantably*. *Tu sais ce que je veux dire.* I used them to round off something—didn't I? Is that quite my game? No, it's not. It's not quite the kind of truth I'm after. Now for *Susannah*. All must be *deeply felt.*

But what is one to do, with this wretched cat and mouse act? There's my difficulty! I must try to write this afternoon instead. There is no reason why I shouldn't! No reason, except the after-effects of pain on a weakened organism.

July 23. Finished *An Ideal Family* yesterday. It seems to me better than *The Doves*, but still it's not good enough. I worked at it hard enough, God knows, and yet I didn't get the deepest truth out of the idea, even once. What *is* this feeling? I feel again that this kind of knowledge is too easy for me; it's even a kind of trickery. I know so much more. This looks and smells like a story, but I wouldn't buy it. I don't want to possess it—to live with it. NO. Once I have written two more, I shall tackle something different—a long story: *At the Bay*, with more difficult relationships. That's the whole problem.

'Out of the pocket of the mackintosh she took an ample bag, which she opened and peered into and shook. Her eyebrows were raised, her lips pressed together....'

'And a very long shining blue-black hairpin gleaming on the faded carpet....'

'She shuddered. And now when she looked at his photograph, even the white flower in his buttonhole looked as though it were made of a curl of mutton-fat...'

'And she saw Mr. Bailey in a blue apron standing at the back of one of those horrible shops. He had one hand on his hip, the other grasped the handle of a long knife that was stuck into a huge chopping block. At the back of him there hung a fringe of small rabbits, their feet tied together, a dark clot of blood trembling from their noses....'

July 18. The noise in this house this morning is sheer hell. It has gone on steadily since shortly after six o'clock, and for some reason the maid seems to have completely lost her head. It's now nearly ten, and she hasn't cleared the breakfast away. I have to go again to the Palace at 11, and the consequence is I'm rather nervous anyway. And I've had the flowers to do and various things to see to like—laundry. I can hardly bear it. Now she plods up. Bang! She will be at the door in a moment. I don't know how to stand it if it goes on. She's here. She's about to put the things in the lift. What are her thoughts? I don't know or care. But I bitterly long for a little private room where I can work undisturbed. The balcony is not good enough; neither is this *salon*. Here again, J. has beaten me. And it's not half so important for him. . . .

A Welcome.

And because, when you arrive unexpected, there is so often a cold gleam in the hussif's eye which means: 'I can manage the sheets perfectly, but the blankets are certainly going to be a problem,' I would have you met in the doorway by a young creature carrying a not too bright lamp, it being, of course, late evening, and chanting, as you brush under the jasmine porch:

> Be not afraid, the house is full of blankets,
> Red ones and white ones, lovely beyond dreaming,
> Key-pattern, tasselled, camel-hair and woolly,
> Softer than sleep or the bosom of a swan.

[In the middle of the manuscript of *Her First Ball*.]

July 25. All this! All that I write—all that I am—is on

the border of the sea. It's a kind of playing. I want to put *all* my force behind it, but somehow, I *cannot!*

> Ful gay was al the ground, and queynt,
> And poudred as men had it peynt
> With many a fresh and sondry flour
> That casten up ful good savour.

[From an unposted letter.]

It's a chill, strange day. I can just get about. I decided this morning to write to S . . . about the Swiss Spahlinger treatment: whether it would be suitable for me, etc. And I shall wire you to-morrow, asking you to go and see S . . .. Say what you like. But let him know that I am practically a hopeless invalid. I have tried to explain about money to him; why I haven't paid him, and I have promised to pay the first moment I can. . . .

August. 'I have been writing a story about an old man.'

She looked vague. 'But I don't think I like old men— do you?' said she. 'They *exude* so.'

This horrified me. It seemed so infernally petty, and more than that . . . it was the saying of a vulgar little mind.

Later: I think it was shyness.

August 11. I don't know how I may write this next story. It's so difficult. But I suppose I shall. The trouble is I am so infernally cold.

[The 'next story' was *The Voyage.* The finished manuscript is dated August 14, 1921.]

[From an unposted letter.]

I would have written a card before, but I have been —am—ill, and to-day's the first day I've taken a pen even so far. I've had an attack of what the doctor calls acute enteritis. I think it was poisoning. Very high fever and sickness and dysentery and so on. *Horrible.* I decided yesterday to go to the Palace, but to-day makes me feel I'll try and see it out here. J. is awfully kind in the menial offices of nurse, and I've not been able to take any food except warm milk, so Ernestine can't work her worst on me. She seems, poor creature, to be much more stupid than ever! Burns everything! Leaves us without eggs, and went off for her afternoon yesterday without a word. We didn't even know she was gone.

Love.

August. A sudden idea of the relationship between 'lovers'.

We are neither male nor female. We are a compound of both. I choose the male who will develop and expand the male in me; he chooses me to expand the female in him. Being made 'whole'. Yes, but that's a process. By love serve ye one another. . . . And why I choose *one* man for this rather than many is for safety. We bind ourselves within a ring and that ring is as it were a wall against the outside world. It is our refuge, our shelter. Here the tricks of life will not be played. Here is *safety* for us to *grow*.

Why, I talk like a child!

August 29. 'If I could only sweep all my garden up the hill, to your doors!' Her perfect little gesture as she said this.

The Candlestick.

[An imaginary letter.]

Many thanks for your stuffy letter. As for the candlestick, dear, if you remember, I gave it you on your last birthday. No wonder it reminded you of me. I have kept it in its paper and intend to return it to you with a pretty little note on your next. Or shall I first send it to you as an early Christmas present and do you return it as a late one or a New Year's gift. Easter we shall leave out. It would be a trifle excessive at Easter. I wonder which of us will be in possession of it at the last. If it is on my side, I shall leave it you in my will, all proper, and I think it would be nice of you, Camilla, to desire that it should be buried with you. Besides, one's mind faints at the idea of a candlestick whirling through space and time for ever—a *fliegende* candlestick, in fact!

I have been suffering from wind round the heart. Such a tiresome complaint, but not dangerous. Really, for anything to be so painful I think I would prefer a spice of danger added. The first act was brought on by a fit of laughing.

September. September is different from all other months. It is more magical. I feel the strange chemical change in the earth which produces mushrooms is the cause, too, of this extra 'life' in the air—a resilience, a sparkle. For days the weather has been the same. One wakes to see the trees outside bathed in green-gold light. It's fresh—not cold. It's clear. The sky is a light pure blue. During the morning the sun gets hot. There is a haze over the mountains. Occasionally a squirrel appears, runs up the mast of a pine tree, seizes a cone and sits in the crook of a branch, holding it like a banana. Now and again a little bird, hanging upside-down, pecks at the seed. There is a constant sound of bells from the valley. It keeps on all day, from early to late.

Midday—with long shadows. Hot and still. And yet there's always that taste of a berry rather than scent of a flower in the air. But what can one say of the afternoons? Of the evening? The rose, the gold on the mountains, the quick mounting shadows? But it's soon cold—Beautifully cold, however.

September.

[The following occurs in the middle of an unpublished and un-finished MS. called 'By Moonlight'. 'Karori' was the 'novel' of which *Prelude* and *At the Bay* were—at one time—to have formed parts. But eventually the idea was abandoned, because K.M. saw

that her 'novel' would have been so unlike a novel that it was no
use calling it one.]

I am stuck beyond words, and again it seems to me
that what I am doing has *no form!* I ought to finish my
book of *stories first* and then, when it's gone, really get
down to my novel, *Karori.*

Why I should be so passionately determined to
disguise this, I don't quite know. But here I lie, pretending, as Heaven knows how often I have before, to write.
Supposing I were to give up this pretence and really
did try? Supposing I only wrote half a page in a
day—it would be half a page to the good; and I should
at least be training my mind to get into the habit of
regular performance. As it is, every day sees me
further off my goal. *And*, once I had this book finished,
I'm free to start the real one. *And* it's a question of
money.

But my idea, even of the short story, has changed
rather, lately—That was lucky! J. opened the door
softly and I was apparently really truly engaged. . . .
And—no, enough of this. It has served its purpose. It
has put me on the right lines.

[At the end of the same MS. is this note.]

This isn't bad, but at the same time it's not good.
It's too easy. . . . I wish I could go back to N.Z. for a
year. But I can't possibly just now. I don't see why
not, in two years' time though.

October 13. Dear *Friend*. I like your criticism. It is
right you should have hated those things in me. For I
was careless and false. I was not *true* in those days. But
I have been trying for a long time now to 'squeeze the
slave out of my soul.' . . . I just want to let you know.

Oh, I am in the middle of a nice story [*The Garden
Party*]. I wish you would like it. I am writing it in this
exercise book, and just broke off for a minute to write
to you.

Thank you for the address. I can't go to Paris before
the spring, so I think it would be better if I did not
write until then. I feel this light treatment is the right
one. Not that I am ill at present. I am not in the least
an invalid, in any way.

It's a sunny, windy day—beautiful. There is a soft
roaring in the trees and little birds fly up into the air
just for the fun of being tossed about.

Good-bye. I press pour hand. Do you dislike the
idea we should write to each other from time to time?

KATHERINE.

[At the end of the manuscript of *The Garden Party*.]

This is a moderately successful story, and that's all.
It's somehow, in the episode at the lane, scamped.

The New Baby

It is late night, very dark, very still. Not a star to be
seen. And now it has come on to rain. What happiness

it is to listen to rain at night; joyful relief, ease; a lapping-round and hushing and brooding tenderness, all are mingled together in the sound of the fast-falling rain. God, looking down upon the rainy earth, sees how faint are these lights shining in little windows,—how easily put out. . . .

Suddenly, quick hard steps mount the stone staircase. Someone is hurrying. There is a knock at my door, and at the same moment a red beaming face is thrust in, as Ernestine announces, 'He is born.'

Born!

'He is born!'

Oh, Ernestine, don't turn away. Don't be afraid. Let me weep too.

You ought to keep this, my girl, just as a *warning* to show what an arch-wallower you *can* be.

October 16. Another radiant day. J. is typing my last story, *The Garden Party*, which I finished on my birthday [October 14]. It took me nearly a month to 'recover' from *At the Bay*. I made at least three false starts. But I could not get away from the sound of the sea, and Beryl fanning her hair at the window. These things would not *die down*. But now I'm not at all sure about that story. It seems to me it's a little 'wispy'—not what it might have been. The *G.P.* is better. But that is not *good enough*, either. . . .

The last few days what one notices more than

anything is the blue. Blue sky, blue mountains, all is a heavenly blueness! And clouds of all kinds—wings, soft white clouds, almost hard little golden islands, great mock-mountains. The gold deepens on the slopes. In fact, in sober fact, it is perfection.

But the late evening is the time—of times. Then with that unearthly beauty before one it is not hard to realize how far one has to go. To write something that will be worthy of that rising moon, that pale light. To be 'simple' enough, as one would be simple before God. . . .

October 27. Stories for my new book.

N.Z. *Honesty:* The Doctor, Arnold Cullen, and his wife Lydia, and Archie the friend.

L. *Second Violin:* Alexander and his friend in the train. Spring—spouting rain. *Wet lilac.*

N.Z. *Six Years After:* A wife and husband on board a steamer. The cold buttons. They see someone who reminds them.

L. *Life like Logs of Driftwood:* This wants to be a long, very well-written story. The men are important, especially the lesser man. It wants a good deal of working . . . newspaper office.

N.Z. *A Weak Heart:* Ronnie on his bike in the evening, with his hands in his pockets, *doing marvels,* by that dark tree at the corner of May Street. Edie and Ronnie.

L. *Widowed:* Geraldine and Jimmie: a house overlooking Sloane Street and Square. Wearing those buds at her heart. 'Married or not married. . . .' From Autumn to Spring.

N.Z. *Our Maude:* Husband and wife play duets and a *one* a *two* a *three* a one a *two three one!* His white waistcoats. Wifeling and Mahub! What a girl you are!

N.Z. *At Karori:* The little lamp. I seen it. And then they were silent. (*Finito:* October 30, 1921.)

I wish that *my* silence were only a two-minute one!

October. I wonder why it should be so very difficult to be humble. I do not think I am a good writer; I realize my faults better than anyone else could realize them. I know exactly where I fail. And yet, when I have finished a story and before I have begun another, I catch myself *preening* my feathers. It is disheartening. There seems to be some bad old pride in my heart; a root of it that puts out a thick shoot on the slightest provocation. . . . This interferes very much with work. One can't be calm, clear, good as one must be, while it goes on. I look at the mountains, I try to pray and I think of something *clever.* It's a kind of excitement within, which shouldn't be there. Calm yourself. Clear yourself. And anything that I write in this mood will be no good; it will be full of *sediment.* If I were well, I would go off by myself somewhere and sit under a tree. One must learn, one must practise, to *forget* oneself. I can't tell the truth about Aunt Anne unless I am free to look into her life without self-consciousness.

Oh God! I am divided still. I am bad. I fail in my personal life. I lapse into impatience, temper, vanity, and so I fail as thy priest. Perhaps poetry will help.

I have just thoroughly cleaned and attended to my fountain-pen. If after this it leaks, then it is *no* gentleman!

November 13. It is time I started a new journal. Come, my unseen, my unknown, let us talk together. Yes, for the last two weeks I have written scarcely anything. I have been idle; I have *failed*. Why? Many reasons. There has been a kind of confusion in my consciousness. It has seemed as though there was no time to write. The mornings, if they are sunny, are taken up with sun-treatment; the post eats away the afternoon. And at night I am tired.

'But it all goes deeper.' Yes, you are right. I haven't been able to yield to the kind of contemplation that is necessary. I have not felt pure in heart, not humble, not good. There's been a stirring-up of sediment. I look at the mountains and I see nothing but mountains. Be frank! I read rubbish. I give way about writing letters. I mean I refuse to meet my obligations, and this of course weakens me in every way. Then I have broken my promise to review the books for *The Nation*. Another *bad spot*. Out of hand? Yes, that describes it— dissipated, vague, not *positive*, and above all, above everything, not working as I should be working— wasting time.

Wasting time. The old cry—the first and last cry—
Why do ye tarry? Ah, why indeed? My deepest desire
is to be a writer, to have 'a body of work' done. And
there the work is, there the stories wait for me, *grow
tired*, wilt, fade, because I will not come. And I hear
and I *acknowledge* them, and still I go on sitting at the
window, playing with the ball of wool. What is to be
done?

I must make another effort—at once. I must begin all
over again. I must try and write simply, fully, freely,
from my heart. *Quietly*, caring nothing for success or
failure, but just going on.

I must keep this book so that I have a record of what
I do each week. (Here a word. As I re-read *At the Bay*
in proof, it seemed to me flat, dull, and not a success at
all. I was very much ashamed of it. I am.) But now to
resolve! And especially to keep in touch with Life—
with the sky and this moon, these stars, these cold,
candid peaks.

November 16. To go to Sierre, if it goes on like this . . .
or to—or to—

November 21. Since then [*i.e.* since writing the entry of
October 16, 1921] I have only written *The Doll's House*.
A bad spell has been on me. I have begun two stories,[1]
but then I told them and they felt betrayed. It is
absolutely fatal to give way to this temptation. . . .

[1] Fragments of these two stories, *Widowed* and *Second Violin*,
and of *Weak Heart*, are in the 'Doves' Nest'.

To-day I began to write, seriously, *The Weak Heart*—a story which fascinates me *deeply*. What I feel it needs so peculiarly is a very subtle variation of 'tense' from the present to the past and back again—and softness, lightness, and the feeling that all is in bud, with a play of humour over the character of Ronnie. And the feeling of the Thorndon Baths, the wet, moist, oozy . . . no, I know how it must be done.

May I be found worthy to do it! Lord, make me crystal clear for thy light to shine through!

November 24. These last days I have been awfully rebellious. Longing for something. I feel uprooted. I want things that J. can so easily do without, that aren't natural to him. I long for them. But then, stronger than all these desires, is the other, which is to *make good* before I do anything else. The sooner the books are written, the sooner I shall be well, the sooner my wishes will be in sight of fulfilment. That is sober truth, of course. As a pure matter of fact I consider this enforced confinement here as God-given. But, on the other hand, I must make the most of it quickly. It is not unlimited any more than anything else is. Oh, why —oh, why isn't anything unlimited? Why am I troubled every single day of my life by the nearness of death and its inevitability? I am really diseased on that point. And I can't speak of it. If I tell J. it makes him unhappy. If I don't tell him, it leaves me to fight it. I am tired of the battle. No one knows how tired.

To-night, when the evening star shone through the side-window and the mountains were so lovely, I sat there thinking of death. Of all there was to do—of Life, which is so lovely—and of the fact that my body is a prison. But this state of mind is *evil*. It is only by acknowledging that I, being what I am, had to suffer *this* in order to do the work I am here to perform. It is only by acknowledging it, by being thankful that work was not taken away from me, that I shall recover. I am weak where I must be strong.

And to-day—Saturday—less than ever. But no matter. I have progressed . . . a little. I have realized *what* it is to be done—the strange barrier to be crossed from thinking it to writing it. . . , Daphne.

[On the next page begins the unfinished MS. of *Daphne*, included in 'The Doves' Nest'.]

SHAKESPEARE NOTES.

All's Well that Ends Well.

The First Lord is worth attending to. One could have thought that his speeches and those of the Second Lord would have been interchangeable; but he is a very definite, quick-cut character. Take, for example, the talk between the two in Act IV Scene III. The Second Lord asks him to let what he is going to tell dwell darkly with him.

First Lord: 'When you have spoken it, 'tis dead, and I am the grave of it.'

And then his comment:

'How mightily sometimes we make us comforts of our losses.'

And this is most excellent:

'The web of our life is of a mingled yarn, good and ill together; our virtues would be proud if our faults whipped them not; and our faults would despair if they were not cherished by our virtues.'

I like the temper of that extremely—and does it not reveal the man? Disillusioned and yet—amused—worldly, and yet he has feeling. But I see him as—quick, full of Life, and marvellously at his ease with his company, his surroundings, his own condition, and the whole small, solid earth. He is like a man on shipboard who is inclined to straddle just to show (but not to *show off*) how well his sea-legs serve him. . . .

The Clown—'a shrewd knave and an unhappy'—comes to tell the Countess of the arrival of Bertram and his soldiers.

'Faith, there's a dozen of 'em, with delicate fine hats and most courteous feathers, that bow and nod the head at every man.'

In that phrase there is all the charm of soldiers on prancing, jingling, dancing horses. It is a veritable little pageant. With what an air the haughty (and intolerable) Bertram wears his two-pile velvet patch—with what disdain his hand in the white laced French glove tightens upon the tight rein of his silver charger. Wonderfully sunny, with a little breeze. And the Clown, of course, sees the humour of this conceit. . . .

Parolles is a lovable creature, a brave little cock-sparrow of a ruffian.

. . . 'I am now, sir, muddied in Fortune's mood, and smell somewhat strong of her strong displeasure.'

I must say Helena is a terrifying female. Her virtue, her persistence, her pegging away after the odious Bertram (and disguised as a pilgrim—so typical!) and then telling the whole story to that *good* widow-woman! And that tame fish Diana. As to lying in Diana's bed and enjoying the embraces meant for Diana—well, I know nothing more sickening. It would take a respectable woman to do such a thing. The worst of it is I can so well imagine . . . for instance acting in precisely that way, and giving Diana a present afterwards. What a cup of tea the widow and D. must have enjoyed while it was taking place, or did D. at the last moment want to cry off the bargain? But to forgive such a woman! Yet Bertram would. There's an espèce de mothers-boyisme in him which makes him stupid enough for anything.

The Old King is a queer old card—he seems to have a mania for bestowing husbands. As if the one fiasco were not enough, Diana has no sooner explained herself than he begins:

> 'If thou be'st yet a fresh uncropped flower
> Choose thou thy husband, and I'll pay thy dower.'

I think Shakespeare must have seen the humour of that. It just—at the very last moment of the play, puts breath into the old fool.

Hamlet.

Coleridge on Hamlet. 'He plays that subtle trick of pretending to act only when he is very near being what he acts.'

... So do we all begin by acting and the nearer we are to what we would be the more perfect our *disguise*. Finally there comes the moment when *we are no longer acting;* it may even catch us by surprise. We may look in amazement at our no longer borrowed plumage. The two have merged; that which we put on has joined that which was; acting has become action. The soul has accepted this livery for its own after a time of trying on and approving.

To act ... to see ourselves in the part—to make a larger gesture than would be ours in life—to declaim, to pronounce, to even exaggerate, to persuade ourselves (?) or others (?). To put ourselves in heart? To do more than is necessary in order that we may accomplish ce qu'il faut.

And then Hamlet is lonely. The solitary person always acts.

But I could write a thousand pages about Hamlets.

Mad Scene. If one looks at it with a cold eye is really very poor. It depends entirely for its effect upon wispy Ophelia. The cardboard King and Queen are of course only lookers-on. They don't care a halfpenny. I think the Queen is privately rather surprised at a verse or two of her songs. ... And who can believe that a solitary violet withered when that silly fussy old pomposity died? And who can believe that Ophelia really loved him, and wasn't thankful to think how peaceful breakfast would be without his preaching?

The Queen's speech after Ophelia's death is exasperating to one's sense of poetic truth. If no one saw it happen—if she wasn't found until she was drowned, how does the Queen know how it happened? Dear Shakespeare has been to the Royal Academy ... for his picture.

Miranda and Juliet.

To say that Juliet and Miranda might very well be one seems to me to show a lamentable want of perception. Innocent, early-morning-of-the-world Miranda, that fair island still half dreaming in a golden haze—lapped about with little joyful hurrying waves of love. ... And small, frail Juliet, leaning upon the dark—a flower that is turned to the moon and closes, reluctant, at chill dawn. It is not even her Spring. It is her time for dreaming: too soon for love. There is a Spring that comes before the real Spring and so there is a love—a false Love. It is incarnate in Juliet.

Romeo and Juliet.

When the old nurse cackles of leaning against the dove-house wall it's just as though a beam of sunlight struck through the curtains and discovered her sitting there in the warmth with a tiny staggerer. One positively feels the warmth of the sunny wall. ...

Twelfth Night.

Malvolio's 'or . . . play with some rich jewel.' There speaks the envious servant-heart that covets his master's possessions. I see him stroking the cloth with a sigh as he puts away his master's coat—holding up to the light or to his fingers the jewel before he snaps it into its ivory case. I see the servant copying the master's expression as he looks in the master's mirror.

And that . . .'having risen from a day bed where I have left Olivia sleeping.' Oh, doesn't that reveal the thoughts of all those strange creatures who attend upon the lives of others!

Anthony and Cleopatra.

Act I. Scene I.

'The triple pillars of the world . . .'
'The wide arch of the ranged empire . . .'
'To-night we'll wander through the streets and note
The qualities of people.' (That is so *true* a pleasure of lovers.)

Act I. Scene 2.

'A Roman thought hath struck him . . .'
'Ah, then we bring forth weeds
When our quick minds lie still . . .'

Enobarbus constantly amazes me, *e.g.* his first speeches with Anthony about Cleopatra's celerity in dying.

'Your old smock brings forth a new petticoat.'

Act I. Scene 3. Like Scene 2. (1) 'Saw you my lord?'

(2) 'Where is he?' The *married* woman. There's jealousy! And then her fury that he's not more upset at Fulvia's death! 'Now I know how you'll behave when I die!'

These are beautiful lines of Anthony's:

'Our separation so abides and flies
That thou, residing here, goest yet with me,
And I, hence fleeing, here remain with thee.'

Act I. Scene 4.

'Like to a vagabond flag upon the stream
Goes to and back, lackeying the varying tide
To rot itself with motion.'

Marvellous words! I can apply them. There is a short story. And then it seems that the weed gets caught up and it sinks; it is gone out to sea and lost. But comes a day, a like tide, a like occasion, and it reappears more sickeningly rotten still! Shall he? Will he? Are there any letters? No letters? The post? Does he miss me? No. Then sweep it all out to sea. Clear the water for ever! Let me write this one day.

'His cheek so much as lanked not.' (Economy of utterance.)

Act III. The short scene between Anthony and the Soothsayer is very remarkable. It explains the tone of Cæsar's remarks to Anthony. . . . And Anthony's concluding speech shows his uneasiness at the truth of it. He'll go to Egypt. He'll go where his weakness is praised for strength. There's a hankering after Egypt between the lines.

Scene 5. 'Tawny-finned fishes . . . their shiny jaws...'
and the adjectives seem part of the nouns when Shakespeare uses them. They grace them so beautifully, attend
and adorn so modestly, and yet with such skill. It so
often happens with lesser writers that we are more
conscious of the servants than we are of the masters,
and quite forget that their office is to serve, to enlarge,
to amplify the power of the master.

'Ram thou thy fruitful tidings in my ears
That long time have been barren.'

Good lines! And another example of the choice of the
place of words. I suppose it was instinctive. But 'fruitful' seems to be just where it ought to be, to be resolved
(musically speaking) by the word 'barren'. One reads
'fruitful' expecting 'barren' almost from the 'sound-
sense'.

'"But yet" is as a jailor to bring forth
Some monstrous malefactor.'

There's matter indeed! Does not that give the pause
that always follows those hateful words. 'But yet'—and
one waits. And both look towards the slowly opening
door. What is coming out? And sometimes there's a
sigh of relief after. Well, it was nothing so very awful.
The gaol-mouse, so to speak, comes mousing through
and cleans his face with his paw.

'I am pale, Charmian.'

Reminds me of Mary Shelley. 'Byron had never seen anyone so pale as I.'

> 'Since I myself
> Have given myself the cause.'

What does that mean exactly? That she sent Anthony away? or let Anthony go?

> 'In praising Anthony I have dispraised Cæsar . . .
> I am paid for it now.'

A creature like Cleopatra always expects to be paid for things.

JANUARY 1. I DREAMED I SAILED TO EGYPT WITH Grandma—a very white boat.

Cold, still. The gale last night has blown nearly all the snow off the trees; only big, frozen-looking lumps remain. In the wood where the snow is thick, bars of sunlight lay like pale fire.

I have left undone those things I ought to have done and I have done those things which I ought not to have done, *e.g.* violent impatience with L.M.

Wrote *The Doves' Nest* this afternoon. I was in no mood to write; it seemed impossible. Yet when I had finished three pages, they were all right. This is a proof (never to be too often proved) that once one has thought out a story nothing remains but the *labour*.

Wing Lee[1] disappeared for the day. Read W.J.D.'s poems. I feel very near to him in mind.

I want to remember how the light fades from a room —and one fades with it, is *expunged*, sitting still, knees together, hands in pockets. . . .

January 2. Little round birds in the fir tree at the side window, scouring the tree for food. I crumbled a piece of bread, but though the crumbs fell in the branches only two found them. There was a strange remoteness

---

[1] Wing Lee, alias Wingley, was K.M.'s little black and white cat. Wing Lee was his original name. It was taken from one of K.M.'s large repertory of comic songs: 'Wing Lee bought a clock the other day, Just because it kept rag-time . . .'

in the air, the scene, the winter cheeping. In the evening, for the first time for . . . I felt rested. I sat up in bed and discovered I was singing within. Even the sound of the wind is different. It is joyful, not ominous and black. Dark looks in at the window and is only black dark. In the afternoon it came on to rain, long glancing rain, falling aslant.

I have not done the work I should have done. I shirk the lunch party [see *The Doves' Nest*]. This is very bad. In fact I am disgusted with myself. There must be a change from now on. What I chiefly admire in Jane Austen is that what she promises, she performs, *i.e.* if Sir T. is to arrive, we have his arrival at length, and it's excellent and exceeds our expectations. This is rare; it is also my very weakest point. Easy to see why. . . .

January 3. I dreamed I was at the Strand Palace—having married M.D.—big blonde—in quantities of white satin. . . .

There was a great deal more snow this morning; it was very soft, 'like wool'. The cocoanut was bought and sawn in half and hung from J.'s balcony. The milk came tinkling out of the nut in brightest drops—not white milk. This was a profound surprise. The flesh of the nut is very lovely—so pure white. But it was that dewy, sweet liquid which made the marvel. Whence came it? It took one to the island.

I read *The Tempest*. The papers came. I over-read them. Tell the truth. I did no work. In fact I was more idle and hateful than ever. Full of sin. Why? 'Oh self, oh self, wake from thy common sleep.' And the worst of it is I feel so much better in health. It is shameful! *The Tempest* seems to me astonishing this time. When one reads the same play again, it is never the same play.

January 4. Dreamed of M.S. An important dream; its tone was important. That gallery over the sea and my 'Isn't it beautiful?' and his weary 'No doubt'. His definition of the two kinds of women. . . .

But I was not so wicked to-day. I have read a good deal of *Cosmic Anatomy* and understood it far better. Yes, such a book does fascinate me. Why does J. hate it so?

To get a glimpse of the relation of things—to follow that relation and find it remains true through the ages enlarges my little mind as nothing else does. It's only a greater view of psychology. It helps me with my writing, for instance, to know that hot + bun may mean Taurus, Pradhana, substance. No, that's not really what attracts me; it's that reactions to certain causes and effects always have been the same. It wasn't for nothing Constantia[1] chose the moon and water, for instance!

Read Shakespeare. The snow is thicker, it clings to the branches like white new-born puppies.

January 5. A long typical boat dream. I was, as usual, going to N.Z. But for the first time my stepmother was *very* friendly—so nice. I loved her. A tragic dream

[1] One of the sisters in *The Daughters of the late Colonel*.

as regards L.M. She disappeared, and it was too late to find her or tell her to come back *at last*.

Read *Cosmic Anatomy*. I managed to work a little. Broke through. This is a great relief. J. and I put out food for the birds. When I went to the window all the food was gone, but there was the tiny print of their feet on the sill. J. brought up the half cocoanut and sprinkled crumbs as well. Very soon, terrified, however, one came, then another, then a third, balanced on the cocoanut. They are precious little atoms.

It still snows. I think I hate snow, downright hate it. There is something stupefying in it, a kind of 'You must be worse before you're better,' and down it spins. I love, I long for the fertile earth. How I have longed for the South of France this year! So do I now.

Soundly rated L.M. about food and clothing. She has a food 'complex'. J. and I read *Mansfield Park* with great enjoyment. I wonder if J. is as content as he appears? It seems too good to be true.

January 6. The first quarter of the Moon. *Jour de fête*. The Christmas Tree is dismantled.

I had a very bad night and did not fall deeply asleep enough to dream.

In the morning, all white, all dim and cold, and snow still falling. While waiting in my room I watched the terrific efforts of a little bird to peck through the ice and get at the sweet food of the nut. He succeeded. But why must he so strive?

My heart is always bad to-day. It is the cold. It feels congested, and I am uneasy, or rather my body is—vile feeling. I cough.

Read Shakespeare, read *Cosmic Anatomy*, read The Oxford Dictionary. Wrote. But nothing like enough.

In the afternoon W ... came to tea. I suspect he is timid, fearful and deeply kind. Deep within that vast substance lurks the *seed*. That is not sentimental. He wished me sun as he left. I felt his wish had power and was a blessing. One can't be mistaken in such things. He *is* in his stockings—pea-green and red! J. came up after ski-ing, excessively handsome—a glorious object, no less. I never saw a more *splendid* figure.

I am wearing my ring on my middle finger as a reminder not to be so base. We shall see. . . .

January 7. It ceased snowing, and a deep, almost gentian blue sky showed. The snow lay heaped on the trees, big blobs of snow, like whipped cream. It was very cold, but, I suppose, beautiful. I cannot see this snow as anything but hateful. So it is.

My birds have made a number of little attacks on the cocoanut, but it is still frozen. I read *Cosmic Anatomy*, Shakespeare and the Bible. Jonah. Very nice about the gourd, and also on his journey, 'paying the fare thereof'.

I wrote at my story, but did not finish the lunch party as I ought to have done. How *very* bad this is!

Had a long talk with L.M. and suddenly saw her again as a figure in a story. She resolves into so many. I could write *books* about her alone!

I dreamed a long dream. Chummie was young again, so was Jeanne. Mother was alive. We were going through many strange rooms—up in lifts, alighting in lounges. It was all vaguely foreign.

January 8. All night dreamed of visiting houses, bare rooms, No. 39, going up and down in lifts, etc.

Heavily, more heavily than ever, falls the snow. It is hypnotizing. One looks, wonders vaguely how much has fallen and how much will fall and—looks again. Bandaged J.'s fingers. The *Mercury* came with *At the Bay*. I am *very* unsatisfied.

In the afternoon J. and I played cribbage, with nuts for counters. I recalled the fact that I used to play so often with such intense—Heavens with what feelings! —in the drawing-room at Carlton Hill while T... played the piano. But it meant absolutely *nothing*. J. giving me a bad nut and me paying him the bad nut again was all that really mattered.

After tea we knitted and talked and then read. We were idle—snow-bound. One feels there is nothing to be done while this goes on.

Had a letter from *The Sketch* asking for work. I must obey. J. and I talked Paris yesterday and he quite understood. This is a proof that one must *be calm and explain* and be TRUE. Remember that!

January 9. Snow. The vegetable garden fence was all but gone. H . . . came and said there was between 6-7 feet of snow. He was very cheerful and friendly. Off his guard, speaking of Miss S . . . he declared, 'Well, the fact is she is not normal. And anyone who is not normal I call *mad*. She is unconventional, that is to say, and people who are that are no good to anyone except themselves.' When he said 'mad', a look came into his eyes—a flash of power—and he swung the stethoscope, then picked up my fan and rattled it open.

Read and knitted and played cards. A long letter from S. I want to believe all he says about my story. He *does* see what I meant. He does not see it as a set of trivial happenings just thrown together. This is enough to be deeply grateful for—more than others will see. But I have this continual longing to write something with all my power, all my force in it.

January 10. Dreamed I was back in New Zealand.

Got up to-day. It was fine. The sun shone and melted the last trace of snow from the trees, from the roof. The drops were not like rain-drops, but bigger, softer, more exquisite. They made one realize how one loves the fertile earth and hates this snow-bound cold substitute.

The men worked outside on the snowy road, trying to raise the telegraph pole. Before they began they had lunch out of a paper, sitting astride the pole. It is very beautiful to see people sharing food. Cutting bread and passing the loaf, especially cutting bread in that age-old way, with a clasp-knife. Afterwards one got up in a tree and sat among the branches working from there, while the other lifted. The one in the tree turned into a kind of bird, as all people do in trees—chuckled, laughed out, peered from among the branches, careless. *At-tend! Ar-rêt! Al-lez!*

January 11. In bed again. Heard from Pinker *The Dial* has taken *The Doll's House*. Wrote and finished *A Cup of Tea*. It took about 4-5 hours. In the afternoon M. came. She looked fascinating in her black suit, something between a Bishop and a Fly. She spoke of my 'pretty little story' in the *Mercury*. All the while she was here I was conscious of a falsity. We said things we meant; we were sincere, but at the back there was nothing but falsity. It was very horrible. I do not want ever to see her or hear from her again. When she said she would not come often, I wanted to cry *Finito!* No, she is not my friend.

There is no feeling to be compared with the feeling of having written and finished a story. I did not go to sleep, but nothing mattered. There it was, *new* and complete.

Dreamed last night of a voyage to America.

January 12. A vile cold day. The parcel came from M. But when one compares it with A.'s exquisite coat. . . .

J. and I 'typed'. I hate dictating; but the story still seems to me to be good. Is it?

All the whole time at the back of my mind slumbers not nor sleeps the idea of Paris, and I begin to plan what I will do *when* . . . Can it be true? What shall I do to express my thanks? I want to adopt a Russian baby, call him Anton, and bring him up as mine, with K. for a godfather and Mme. Tchehov for a godmother. Such is my dream.

I don't feel so sinful this day as I did, because I have written something and the tide is still high. The ancient landmarks are covered. Ah! but to write better! Let me write better, more deeply, more largely.

Baleful icicles hang in a fringe outside our window-pane.

January 13. Heard from B. Her letter was almost frightening. It brought back the inexplicable past. It flashed into my mind too that she must have a large number of letters of mine which don't bear thinking about. In some way I fear her. I feared her at the rue de Tournon. There was a peculiar recklessness in her manner and in her tones which made me feel she would recognize no barriers at all. At the same time, of course, one is fascinated.

Wrote to K. Began a new story, but it went too slowly. J. typed for me. I am again held up by letters to write. Letters are the real *curse* of my existence. I hate to write them: I have to. If I don't, there they are—the great guilty gates barring my way.

H. came and suggested my heart condition was

caused by the failure to expand the diaphragm. Then why, in that case, not learn to expand it?

January 14. I got up to-day and felt better. It was intensely cold.

M. came in the afternoon. She and I were alone. She wore a little blue hood fastened under the chin with a diamond clasp. She looked like a very ancient drawing. She suggested that if I did become cured, I might no longer write. . . .

Dreamed last night I was in a ship, with the most superb, unearthly (in the heavenly sense) seas breaking. Deep, almost violet blue waves with high foamy crests, and this white foam bore down on the blue in long curls. It was a marvellous sight. The dream was about Chummie. He had married a girl without permission and Father and Mother were in despair. I 'realized' it was to be; what would have happened if he had not died.

Wingley made a dash at the bird window to-day.

January 15. Dreamed I was shopping, buying under-clothes in Cook's and then in Warnock's.[1] But the dream ended *horribly*.

Another chill, bloodless day. I got up, but all was difficult. In the afternoon J. went down the mountain and came back in the evening with a letter for me

---

[1] These are or were shops in Wellington, N.Z.

from M.; so generous, so sweet a letter that I am ashamed of what I said or thought the other day.

I have worked to-day in discomfort—not half enough. I could have written a whole story. Saw for the first time an exquisite little crested bird. Its call is a trill, a shake, marvellously delightful. It was very shy, though, and never had the courage to stop and eat. Saw people in sleighs and on luges. Snow is very *blue*. The icicles at dawn this morning were the colour of opals—blue lit with fire. M. lent us *Will Shakespeare*. Really awful stuff! I had better keep this for a sign.

January 16. A wonderfully pleasant dream about Paris. All went so well. The Doctor and his friends all had the same atmosphere. It was good, kind, quietly happy. I don't know when I've had a dream more delightful.

But the day has not been delightful. On the contrary. It snowed heavily, it was bitter cold, and my congestion worse than ever. I have been in pain and discomfort all day. My lung creaks. I have done no work. After tea I simply went to sleep out of sheer inertia. I am in a slough of despond to-day, and like everybody in such an ugly place, I am ugly, I feel ugly. It is the triumph of matter over spirit. This must not be. To-morrow at all costs (here I swear) I shall write a story. This is my first resolution . . . in this journal. I dare not break it. Tomlinson's letter to J. came yesterday. It was a beautiful letter and not to be forgotten. But why am I so *bad?*

January 17. Tchehov made a mistake in thinking that if he had had more time he would have written more fully, described the rain, and the midwife and the doctor having tea. The truth is one can get only *so much* into a story; there is always a sacrifice. One has to leave out what one knows and longs to use. Why? I haven't any idea, but there it is. It's always a kind of race to get in as much as one can before it *disappears*.

But time is not really in it. Yet wait. I do not understand even now. I am pursued by time myself. The only occasion when I ever felt at leisure was while writing *The Daughters of the Late Colonel*. And at the end I was so terribly unhappy that I wrote as fast as possible for fear of dying before the story was sent. I should like to prove this, to work at *real leisure*. Only thus can it be done.

January 18. H. is a man to remember. At tea that day. Mrs. M. before the huge silver kettle and pots and large plates. The *ornate* cake; one must remember that cake. 'It seems such a pity to cut it,' and the way the old hand, so calmly, grasped the knife. H. leaning back, slapping two pieces of bread and butter together. 'More tea, Jim?' 'No, thanks. Yes. Half a cup.' Pouring from the kettle to the tea-cup, the fat finger on the knob. 'And how is he?' 'Bleeding like a pig!' 'Oh, dear'—gathering her lace scarf into her lap—'I'm sorry to hear that.'

H. always collects something—always will. China,

silver, 'any old thing that comes along'. He's musical
and collects fiddles. His feeling for his children is so
tender that it's pain. He can't understand it.

One must remember, too, his extraordinary in-
security. The world rocks under him, and it's only
when he has that stethoscope that he can lay down the
law. *Then* lay it down he does. 'What I say is: she's
mad. She's not normal. And a person who isn't normal
I call *mad—barmy.*' And you hear pride in his voice;
you hear the unspoken: 'I am a plain man, you
know. . . .'

I'm afraid there is a vein of tremendous cynicism in
him, too. He feels somewhere that all is ashes. He likes
to go to church, to take part, to sing when others sing,
to kneel, to intone the responses. This puts his heart
at rest. But when it is over and he is at home and there
is a smell of beef, there comes this restlessness. When
he was little, I imagine he pulled the wings off flies.
And I still see suicide as his end, in a kind of melan-
cholia, and 'nobody wants me', and 'damned if I won't'.

January 20. Wrote to de la Mare. Why it should be
such an effort to write to the people one loves I cannot
imagine. It's none at all to write to those who don't
really count. But for weeks I have thought of D.,
wanted to, longed to write to him, but something held
back my pen. What? Once started, really started, all
goes easily. . . . I told him in this letter how much I
thought of him. I suppose it is the effect of isolation

that I can truly say I think of de la Mare, Tchehov, Koteliansky, Tomlinson, Lawrence, Orage, every day. They are part of my life. . . .

I have got more or less used to pain at last. I wonder sometimes if this is worse or better than what has been; but I don't expect to be without. But I have a suspicion—sometimes a certainty—that the real cause of my illness is not my lungs at all, but something else. And if this were found and cured, all the rest would heal.

January 21. Grandma's birthday. Where is that photograph of my dear love leaning against her husband's shoulder, with her hair parted so meekly and her eyes raised? I love it. I long to have it. For one thing Mother gave it me at a time when she loved me. But for another—so much more important—it is *she*, my own Grandma, young and lovely. That arm. That baby sleeve. Even the velvet ribbon. I must see them again.

And one day I must write about Grandma at length, especially of her beauty in her bath—when she was about sixty. Wiping herself with the towel. I remember now how lovely she seemed to me. And her fine linen, her throat, her scent. I have never really described her yet. Patience! The time will come.

January 22. My feeling about Ernestine is shameful. But there it is. Her tread, her look, the way her nose is screwed round, her intense stupidity, her wrists—revolt me. This is *bad*. For she feels it, I am sure she does. When we speak together she blushes in a way that doesn't seem to me natural. I feel that her self-respect is shamed by my thoughts.

Lumbago. This is a very queer thing. So sudden, so painful. I must remember it when I write about an old man. The start to get up—the pause—the look of fury—and how, lying at night, one seems to get *locked*. To move is an agony; till finally one discovers a movement which is possible. But that helpless feeling about with the legs first!

January 23. *Paris?* To remember the sound of wind— the peculiar wretchedness one can feel while the wind blows. Then the warm soft wind of spring searching out the heart. The wind I call the Ancient of Days which blows here at night. The wind that shakes the garden at night when one runs out into it.

Dust. Turning one's back on a high, heavy wind. Walking along the Esplanade when the wind carries the sea over. The wind of summer, so playful, that rocked and swung in the trees here. And wind moving through grass so that the grass quivers. This moves me with an emotion I don't ever understand. I always see a field, a young horse—and there is a very fair Danish girl telling me something about her step-father. The girl's name is Elsa Bagge.

January 24. Wrote and finished *Taking the Veil*. It took me about 3 hours to write finally. But I had been thinking over the *décor* and so on for weeks—nay, months, I believe. I can't say how thankful I am to have been born in N.Z., to know Wellington as I do, and to have it to range about in. Writing about the convent seemed so natural. I suppose I have not been in the grounds more than twice. But it is one of the places that remains as vivid as ever. I must not forget the name of *Miss Sparrow*,[1] nor the name *Palmer*.

January 25. Played cribbage with J. I delight in seeing him win. When we play he sometimes makes faces at me—the same kind of faces that Chummie used to make. I think I am never so fond of him as when he does this.

We were talking of the personality of the cat to-day and saying that we ought to write it down. It is true he has become as real as if he could talk. I feel he does talk, and that when he is silent it is only a case of making his nettle shirt and he will begin. Perhaps the most engaging glimpse of him is playing his fiddle with wool for strings or sitting up to the piano and playing Nelly Bly. But his love Isbel, his whole complete little life side by side with ours, ought to be told. I shall never tell it, though.

January 26. Pinker writes to say *The Nation* has taken 'The Doll's House'.

I am sure that meditation is the cure for the sickness

[1] See entry of October 18, 1920.

of my mind, *i.e.* its lack of control. I have a terribly sensitive mind which receives every impression, and that is the reason why I am so carried away *and* borne under.

January 27. M. came, wearing her woolly lamb. A strange fate overtakes me with her. We seem to be always talking of physical subjects. They bore and disgust me, for I feel it is waste of time, and yet we always revert to them. She lay back on the pillows, talking. She had an absent air. She was saying how fine women were . . . and it was on the tip of my tongue to be indiscreet. But I was not. Thank Heaven!

I have been in pain, in bad pain all day. I ache all over. I can hardly stand. It seems impossible that I am going away on Monday.

January 28. These preparations for flight are almost incredible. The only way to keep calm is to play crib. J. and I sit opposite each other. I feel we are awfully united. And we play and laugh and it seems to keep us together. While the game lasts, we are there. A queer feeling. . . .

January 29. H. came. He says my right lung is practically all right. Can one believe such words? The other is a great deal better. *He* thinks my heart will give me far less trouble at a lower level. Can this be true? He was so hopeful to-day that T.B. seemed no longer a scourge. It seemed that one recovered more often than not. Is this fantastic?

Tidied all my papers. Tore up and ruthlessly destroyed much. This is always a great satisfaction. Whenever I prepare for a journey I prepare as though for death. Should I never return, all is in order. This is what life has taught me.

In the evening I wrote to O. about his book. It has taken me a week to write the letter. J. and I seem to have played cribbage off and on all day. I feel there is much love between us. Tender love. *Let it not change!*

January 30. There was a tremendous fall of snow on Sunday. Monday was the first *real* perfect day of winter. It seemed that the happiness of J. and of me reached its zenith on that day. We could not have been happier; that was the feeling. Sitting one moment on the balcony of the bedroom, for instance, or driving in the sleigh through masses of heaped-up snow. He looked so beautiful, too—hatless, strolling about with his hands in his pockets. He weighed himself. 10 stone. There was a harmonium in the waiting-room. Then I went away, after a quick but not hurried kiss. . . .

It was very beautiful on the way to Sierre. Then I kept wondering if I was seeing it all for the last time— the snowy bushes, the leafless trees. 'I miss the buns.'

January 31. Travelling is terrible. All is so sordid, and the train shatters one. Tunnels are *hell*. I am frightened of travelling.

We arrived in Paris late, but it was very beautiful—
all emerging from water. In the night I looked out and
saw *the men with lanterns*. The hotel all sordid again—
fruit peelings, waste-paper, boots, grime, ill-temper.
In the evening I saw Manoukhin. But on the way there,
nay, even before, I realized my heart was not in it.
I feel divided in myself and angry and without virtue.
Then L.M. and I had one of our famous quarrels, and
I went to the wrong house. Don't forget, as I rang the
bell, the scampering and laughter inside. M. had a
lame girl there as interpreter. He said through her he
could cure me completely. But I did not believe it. It
all seemed suddenly unimportant and ugly. But the
flat was nice—the red curtains, marble clock, and picture
of ladies with powdered hair.

February 1. At 5.30 I went to the *clinique* and saw the
other man, D. I asked him to explain the treatment
and so on. He did so. But first: as I approached the door
it opened and the hall, very light, showed, with the
maid smiling, wearing a little shawl, holding back the
door. Through the hall a man slipped quickly carrying
what I thought was a *cross* of green leaves. Suddenly the
arms of the little cross waved feebly, and I saw it was a
small child strapped to a wooden tray. While I waited,
voices came from another room—very loud voices, M.'s
over and above them: *Da! Da!* and then an inter-
rogatory: *Da?* I have the feeling that M. is a really
good man. I have also a sneaking feeling (I use that

word 'sneaking' advisedly) that he is a kind of unscrupulous impostor. Another proof of my divided nature. All is disunited. Half boos, half cheers.

Yes, that's it. To do anything, to be anything, one must gather oneself together and 'one's faith make stronger'. Nothing of any worth can come from a disunited being. It's only by accident that I write anything worth a rush, and then it's only skimming the top—no more. But remember *The Daughters* [*of the Late Colonel*] was written at Mentone in November when I was not so bad as usual. I was trying with all my soul to be good. Here I try and fail, and the fact of consciousness makes each separate failure very important—each a *sin*. If, combined with M.'s treatment, I treated myself—worked out of this slough of despond —lived an honourable life—and, above all, made straight my relations with L.M. . . . I am a *sham*. I am also an egoist of the deepest dye—such a one that it was very difficult to confess to it in case this book should be found. Even my being well is a kind of occasion for *vanity*. There is nothing worse for the soul than egoism. Therefore . . .

February 3. I went to M. for a treatment. A curious impression remains. M.'s beautiful gesture coming into the room was perfect. But D. shouted so, pushed his face into mine, asked me *indecent* questions. Ah, that's the horror of being ill. One must submit to having one's secrets held up to the light, and regarded with a cold stare. D. is a proper Frenchman. 'Êtes-vous constipée?' Shall I ever forget that, and the wadding of his tie showing over his white coat? M. sits apart, smoking, and his head—which is a curious shape: one is conscious of it all the time as of an instrument—hangs forward. But he is deeply different. He desires to reassure. 'Pas de cavernes.'

Had palpitation from the moment of getting on to the table till 5 o'clock. But when I felt this coming on while rays were working, I felt simply horribly callous. I thought: Well, if this kills me—let it! Voilà! That shows how *bad* I am.

February 4. Massingham accepts the idea of a regular story. Heard from K . . . about 'people'. It was rather a horrible day. I was ill, and at night I had one of my terrible fits of temper over a parcel. Is it possible one can be so unruly?

Heard from J. saying he will stay in Montana. There breathes in his letter the relief from strain. It is remarkable. He does not believe a word about M. and talks of coming to 'fetch' me in May. Well, if I am any better, there will never be any more *fetching*. Of that I am determined. The letter kept me awake until very late. And my sciatica! Put it on record, in case it ever goes, what a pain it is. Remember to give it to someone in a story one day. L.M. is a very tragic figure. Remember her eyes—the pupils dark—black—and her whiteness. Even her hair seems to grow pale. She folded the quilt and held it in her arms as though it was a baby.

February 5. Wrote at my story, read Shakespeare. Read Goethe, thought, prayed.

The day was cold and fine. But I felt ill and could do nothing but lie still all day. This going to Paris has been so much more important than it seemed. Now I begin to see it as the result, the ending of all that reading. I mean that even *Cosmic Anatomy* is involved. Something has been built, a raft, frail and not very seaworthy; but it will serve. Before, I was cast into the water when I was 'alone'—I mean during my illness— and now something supports me. But much is to be done. Much discipline and meditation is needed. Above all, it is important to get work done. Heard from Pinker that Cassells have taken 'A Cup of Tea'.

Thought about French women and their impudent confidence in the power of sex.

February 6. Letters from B. and J. B.'s letter was the most beautiful I have ever received. It gave me a strange shock to find J. never even asked how things were going. A boyish letter like so many I have had, but absolutely impersonal. It might have been written to anyone. True, he was anxious for the post. But . . . that was because he is alone. Do I make J. up? Is he thankful to sink into himself again? I feel relief in every line. There's no strain—nothing that binds him. Then let it continue so. But I will not take a house anywhere. I, too, will be free (I write exactly as I feel). I do not want to see J. again just now. I shall beg him not to come here. He is at present just like a fish that has escaped from the hook.

A bad day. I feel ill, in an obscure way—horrible pains and so on, and weakness. I could do nothing. The weakness was not only physical. I *must heal my Self* before I will be well.

Yes, that is the important thing. No attention is needed here. This must be done alone and at once. It is at the root of my not getting better. My mind is not *controlled*. I idle, I give way, I sink into despair.

February 9. A miserable day. In the night I thought for hours of the evils of uprooting. Every time one leaves anywhere, something precious, which ought not to be killed, is left to die.

February 10. I did not go to the *clinique* because of my chill. Spent the day in bed, reading the papers. The feeling that someone was coming towards me is too strong for me to work. It was like sitting on a bench at the end of a long avenue in a park and seeing someone far in the distance coming your way. She tries to read. The book is in her hand, but it's all nonsense, and might as well be upside down. She reads the advertisements as though they were part of the articles.

I must not forget the long talk L.M. and I had the other evening about *hate*. What is hate? Who has ever described it? Why do I feel it for her? She says: 'It is because I am nothing, I have suppressed all my desires to such an extent that now I have none. I don't think. I don't feel.' I reply: 'If you were cherished and loved for a week, you would recover.' And that is true, and I would like to do it. It seems I ought to do it. But I don't. The marvel is that she understands. No one else on earth could understand.

All that week she had her little corner. 'I may come into my little corner to-night?' she asks timidly, and I reply—so cold, so cynical—'If you want to.' But what would I do if she didn't come?

J. arrived early in the morning. In half an hour it seemed he had been here a long time. I still regret his coming here for *his* sake. I know it is right for our sake. We went together to the *clinique*. Bare leafless trees. A wonderful glow in the sky: the windows flashed fire. M . . . drew a picture of my heart. I wish he had not. I am haunted by the hideous picture, by the thought of my heart like a heavy drop in my breast. But he is good.

February 12. We put the chess-men on the board and began to play. It was an unsettled day. L.M. in and out with no home—no place—whirled like a leaf along this dark passage and then out into the raw street.

J. read the Tchehov aloud. I had read one of the stories myself and it seemed to me nothing. But read aloud, it was a masterpiece. How was that?

I want to remember the evening before. I was asleep. He came in—thrust his head in at the door and *as* I woke, I did not know him. I saw a face which reminded me of his mother and Richard. But I felt a kind of immediate dread confusion. I knew I ought to know it and that it belonged to him, yet he was as it were not present. I think this is what people who are going out of their minds must feel about the faces that bend over them and old, old people about the children. And that accounts for the foolish offended look in their faces sometimes. They feel it's not right they should not know.

February 13. Felt ill all day. Feeling of violent confusion in my body and head. I feel more ill now than ever, so it seems.

J. went out and bought a tea-pot and so on; arranged a game of chess and we started playing. But the pains in my back and so on make my prison almost unendurable. I manage to get up, to dress, to make a show of getting to the restaurant and back without being discovered. But that is literally all. The rest is rather like being a beetle shut in a book, so shackled that one can do nothing but lie down. And even to lie down becomes a kind of agony. The worst of it is I have again lost hope. I don't, I can't believe this will change. I have got off the ship again and am swept here and there by the sea.

February 14. Another hellish day. But J. found some pastilles which help my throat, and it seemed to me they had a calming effect on my heart.

I had one of my perfect dreams. I was at sea, sailing with my parasol opened to just a 'freshet' of wind. Heavenly the sea, the sky, the land—parasol pink—boat pale pink.

If I could only get over my discouragement! But who is going to help with that! Now that L.M. is going I have more to do—all my clothes and so on to put away and pull out, as well as a bowl or two to wash. The effort uses what remains of my strength. By 5 o'clock I am finished and must go to bed again.

It is a very dull day. The canaries sing. I have been reading Bunin's stories. He is not a sympathetic soul, but it is good to read him . . . he carries one away.

February 17. Went to the *clinique*. I felt that all was wrong there. M. was distrait and a little angry. D. as usual sailed over everything. But that means nothing. It seemed to me there had been some trouble or some trouble was brewing.

The servant there is a very beautiful plump woman with a ravishing smile. Her eyes are grey. She curls her hair in a small fringe and she wears a little grey shawl, an apron, and a pair of rather high boots; stepping lightly, with one small plump hand holding the shawl, she opens the door.

February.

[The following is a list of stories, arranged apparently for inclusion in a volume. Those in the second column were already written; those in the first column to be written. Of these only *The Fly* was actually written. Some fragments of the others are printed in 'The Doves' Nest'.]

The Major and the Lady [Widowed?].	A Cup of Tea [January 11, 1922].
The Mother.	Taking the Veil
The Fly.	[January 24, 1922].
An Unhappy Man.	The Doll's House
Lucien.	[October 24-30, 1921].
Down the Sounds.	
A Visit.	
Sisters.	
The New Baby.	
Confidences.	
The Dreamers.	
Aunt Fan.	
Honesty.	
Best Girl.	

February 20. Finished *The Fly*.

May 1. Oh, what will this beloved month bring?

May 3. *Paris*. I must begin writing for Clement Shorter to-day 12 'spasms' of 2,000 words each. I thought of the Burnells, but no, I don't think so. Much better, the Sheridans, the three girls and the brother and the Father and Mother and so on, ending with a long description of Meg's wedding to Keith Fenwick. Well, there's the first flown out of the nest.

The sisters Bead, who come to stay. The white sheet on the floor when the wedding dress is tried on. Yes, I've got the details all right. But the point is—Where shall I begin? One certainly wants to dash.

Meg was playing. I don't think I ought to begin with that. It seems to me the mother's coming home ought to be the first chapter. The other can come later. And in that playing chapter what I want to stress chiefly is: Which is the real life—that or this?—late afternoon, these thoughts—the garden—the beauty—how all things pass—and how the end seems to come so soon.

And then again there is the darling bird—I've always loved birds—Where is the little chap? . . .

What is it that stirs one so? What is this seeking—so joyful—ah, so gentle! And there seems to be a moment when all is to be discovered. Yes, that's the feeling. . . .

The queer thing is I only remember how much I have forgotten when I hear that piano. The garden of the Casino, the blue pansies. But oh, how am I going to write this story?

[There follows the opening paragraph of the story.]

'The late afternoon was beautiful in Port Willin. There was a moment when the whole small town seemed to quiver in those last bright rays. Gold shone the harbour, the windows of the big hospital on Clifton Hill flashed fiery. Only the pigeons flying so high above Post Office Square and the plumes of smoke rising from the evening fires were silver.'

[An unposted letter.]

May. Just a line to say—J. and I both have so much work to do this summer that we have decided when we leave here (end of this month) to go to the Hotel d'Angleterre, Randogne. Does that make you open your eyes? But in the summer, June and July, that place was so lovely and I know it. It would only take a day to settle and a look at the mountains, before we could work. All other arrangements are too difficult— Germany and so on. We have not, literally, the time to discover a new place and take our bearings. Then we shall be near Elizabeth, too. The winter we are going to spend in Bandol at the Beau Rivage. I am going to get a maid now at once. I can't do without one. I simply have not the time to attend to everything and I can't bear, as you know, 'untidiness'.... Don't speak of our plans, by chance, will you?

There is a really superb professional pianist here. He plays nearly all day and writes his own music. Au revoir.   K.M.

[In May K.M. left Paris to spend the summer in Switzerland, her plan then being to return to Paris in October for a second course of the same treatment, which had been (or seemed to the outside observer to have been) successful. When she returned to Switzerland and was examined by her previous doctor, he was astonished at her progress.

But K.M. never believed that she would die of consumption, but always of heart failure, and she thought that her heart had grown worse under the treatment. And, deeper than this, she had come to the conviction that her bodily health depended upon her spiritual condition. Her mind was henceforward preoccupied with discovering some way to 'cure her soul'; and she eventually resolved, to my great regret, to abandon her treatment, and to live as though her grave physical illness were incidental, and even, so far as she could, as though it were non-existent.]

June. Randogne, Switzerland. I find the rapture at being alone hard to understand. Certainly when I am sitting out of sight under a tree I feel I could be content *never to return*. As to 'fear', it is gone. It is replaced by a kind of callousness. What will be, will be. But this is not a very useful statement, for I've never put it to the test.

Should I be as happy with anyone at my side? No. I'd begin to talk, and it's far nicer not to talk. Or, if it were J. he'd open a little blue book by Diderot, *Jacques le Fataliste*, and begin to read it, and that would make me wretched. . . . Why the devil want to read stuffy, snuffy Diderot when there is this other book before one's eyes? I do not want to be a book *worm*. If its book is taken away from it, the little blind head is raised; it wags, hovers, terribly uneasy, in a void—until it begins to burrow again.

Loneliness: 'Oh Loneliness, of my sad heart be Queen!' It isn't in the least that. My heart is not sad except when I am among people, and then I am far too distracted to think about Queens. (Oh, dear! Here is a walking tragedy—Madame with a whole tray of food! And I begged for a bastick, only a bastick!)

[The following description is of a family who lived in a small chalet within view of K.M.'s window at Randogne.]

I have watched this big heavy woman, moving so sullen, plodding in and out with her pails and brushes, coming to the door at midday and evening to look for her husband and child. She looks neither sad nor happy; she looks resigned and stupefied. Sometimes, when she stops and stares round her, she is like a cow that is being driven along a road, and sometimes when, leaning out of the window, she watches her quick husband, so jauntily cutting up logs of wood, I think she hates him—and the sight of her suffocates him.

But to-day, it being the first fine day since the lodgers have come, they went off for a walk and left the nurse-girl in charge of the baby. A 'cradle' made of two straw baskets on trestles was brought out into the sun and the baby *heaped* up in it. Then the nurse-girl disappeared.

Round the side of the house came my woman. She stopped. She looked round quickly. She leaned over the cradle and held out her finger to the baby. Then it seemed she was simply overcome with the loveliness and the wonder of this little thing. She tip-toed round the cradle, bent over, shook her head, shook her finger— pulled up a tiny sleeve, looked at a dimpled arm. Her little girl, in a white hat (in honour of the lodgers) danced up. I imagine my woman asked her how she would like a little brother. And the little girl was fascinated, as small children are by smaller.

'Kiss his hand,' said my woman. She watched her daughter, very serious, kiss the tiny hand; and she could hardly bear that anyone should touch the infant but herself. She snatched her daughter away. . . .

When finally she dragged herself away, she was trembling. She went up the steps into the house, stood in the middle of the kitchen, and it seemed that the child within realized her love and moved. A faint, timid smile was on her lips. She believed and she did not believe.

Gyp, their dog, is the most servile creature imaginable. He is a fat brown and white spaniel with a fat round end of tail which wags for everybody at every moment. His passion is for the baby. If anyone throws him sticks he dashes off and brings them back to lay at the foot of the cradle. When his mistress carries the baby, he dances round them so madly, in such a frenzy of delight, that one doesn't believe in him. He feels himself one of the family—a family dog.

The master is a very stupid conceited fellow with a large thin nose, a tuft of hair, and long thin legs. He walks slowly, holding himself perfectly rigid. He keeps his hands in his pockets always. Yesterday he wore all day a pair of pale blue woollen slippers with tassels. And it was obvious he admired himself in these slippers tremendously. To-day he is walking about in his shirt-

sleeves, wearing a sky-blue shirt. He wears black velvet
trousers and a short coat. I am sure he thinks he is
perfectly dressed for the country. Ah, if he only had
a gun to carry on his shoulder!

When he came home, he walked stiff, rigid like a
post, hands in pockets up to the front door and *stood
there*. Did not knock, gave no sign. In less than a
minute the door opened to him. His wife *felt* he was there.

(What a passion one feels for the sun here!)

The friend is a dashing young man in a grey suit,
with a cap always worn very much on one side. His
cap he does not like to take off. He is the kind of man
who sits on the edge of tables or leans against the
counter of bars with his thumbs in his waistcoat. He
feels a dog. He is sure all the girls are wild about him,
and it's true each time he looks at one, she is ready to
titter. For all his carelessness, he's close with money.
When he and his 'friend' go up to the village for stores,
he lounges in the shop, smells things, *suggests* things,
but turns his back and whistles when it comes to add-
ing up the bill. He thinks the friend's wife is in love
with him.

(When the dog is tied up, it cries pitifully, sobs.
The sound, so unrestrained, *pleases* them.)

The wife is small, untidy, with large gold rings in
her hair. She wears white canvas shoes and a jacket
trimmed with artificial fur. She is the woman who is
spending the day at the seaside. She looks dissatisfied,
unhappy. I am sure she is a terrible muddler.

(The dog is really very hysterical.)

They have a little servant maid of about sixteen, with a loose plait of dark streaky hair and silver-rimmed spectacles. She walks in a terribly meek but self-satisfied way, pushing out her stomach. She is meekness *itself*. How she bows her head and walks after her master! It is terrible to see. She wishes to be invisible, to pass unseen. 'Don't look at me!' And she effaces herself. (This must be written very directly.) She it is who holds the baby. When the others have gone, she rather lords it over the baby, turns up his clothes and exclaims with quite an air.

The baby is at that age when it droops over a shoulder. It is still a boneless baby, blowing bubbles, in a little blue muslin frock. When it cries, it cries as though it were being squeezed. Its feet, in white boots, are like little cakes of dough.

(The dog's enthusiasm is enough to make you want to kick it. When they come out, cold, damp, depressed, there he is leaping, asking when the fun's going to begin. It is sickening.)

A queer bit of psychology: I had to disappear behind the bushes to-day in a hollow. That act made me feel nearer to normal health than I have felt for years. Nobody there; nobody wondered if I was all right, *i.e.* there was nothing to distinguish me, at that moment, from an ordinary human being.

Each little movement of this bird is made so ostentatiously—as if it were trying to show itself off as much as possible. Why?

But to continue with this *alone*-ness—to gather it up a little? Could I . . . ? It seems to me to depend entirely on health in my case. If I were well and could spend the evenings sitting up writing till about eleven. . . .

To look up through the trees to the far-away heavenly blue.

Now it's getting late afternoon and all sounds are softer, deeper. The sough of the wind in the branches is more thoughtful.

This—this is as great happiness as I shall ever know. It is greater happiness than I had ever thought possible. But why is it incompatible with . . . only because of your weakness. There is nothing to prevent you being like this. In fact, don't you yet know that the more active and apart you make your own life, the more content the other is? What he finds intolerable is the lack of privacy. *But so do you.* It makes him feel as though he were living under a vacuum jar. So it does you. You hang on thinking to please him until he longs for you to be gone.

How badly, how stupidly you manage your life! Don't you realize that both of you have had enough contact to last for years, that the only way for each of you to be renewed and refreshed is for you to go apart. Not necessarily to *tear* apart, but to go apart as wisely as possible. You are the most stupid woman I have ever met. You never will see that it all rests with you. If you do not take the initiative, nothing will be done. The reason why you find it so hard to write is because you are learning nothing. I mean of the things that count—like the sight of this tree with its purple cones against the blue. How can I put it, that there is gum on the cones? 'Gemmed?' *No*. 'Beaded?' *No*. 'They are like crystals.' Must I? I am afraid so. . . .

[Towards the end of July K.M., finding the height of Randogne too great a strain on her heart, descended to Sierre.]

July. Sierre. This is a damning little note-book, quite in the old style. How I am committed!

To-day is Tuesday. Since leaving Montana I have written about a page. The rest of the time I seem to have slept! This, of course, started all the Old Fears: that I should never write again, that I was getting sleeping sickness and so on. But this morning I nearly kicked off, and this evening I feel perhaps a time of convalescence was absolutely necessary. The mind was choked with the wrack of all those dreadful tides. I wrote to K . . . to-day. It seems to bring things nearer.

It's only now I am beginning to see again and to re-cognize again the beauty of the world. Take the swallows to-day, their flutter-flutter, their velvet-forked tails, their transparent wings that are like the fins of fishes. The little dark head and breast golden in the light. Then the beauty of the garden, and the beauty of raked paths. . . . Then, the silence.

I wage eternally a war of small deceits. Tear this book up! Tear it up, now! But now I am pretending to be making notes on a book I have already read and despise. . . .

What dreadful, awful rot!

I should like to write the canary story to-morrow. So many ideas come and go. If there is time I shall write them all. If this uninterrupted time continues. The story about this hotel would be wonderful if I could do it.[1]

If there is a book to be read, no matter how bad that book is, I read it. I will read it. Was it always so with me? I don't remember. Looking back, I imagine I was always writing. Twaddle it was, too. But better far write twaddle or anything, anything, than nothing at all.

[At the end of August 1922 K.M. returned to London.]

My first conversation with O. took place on August 30, 1922.

On that occasion I began by telling him how dissatisfied I was with the idea that Life must be a lesser thing than we were capable of imagining it to be. I had the feeling that the same thing happened to nearly everybody whom I knew and whom I did not know. No sooner was their youth, with the little force and impetus characteristic of youth, done, than they

---

[1] *Father and the Girls:* see 'The Doves' Nest', which contains also *The Canary*.

stopped growing. At the very moment that one felt that now was the time to gather oneself together, to use one's whole strength, to take control, to be an adult, in fact, they seemed content to swop the darling wish of their hearts for innumerable little wishes. Or the image that suggested itself to me was that of a river flowing away in countless little trickles over a dark swamp.

They deceived themselves, of course. They called this trickling away—greater tolerance—wider interests —a sense of proportion—so that work did not rule out the possibility of 'life'. Or they called it an escape from all this mind-probing and self-consciousness—a simpler and therefore a better way of life. But sooner or later, in literature at any rate, there sounded an undertone of deep regret. There was an uneasiness, a sense of frustration. One heard, one thought one heard, the cry that began to echo in one's own being: 'I have missed it. I have given up. This is not what I want. If this is all, then Life is not worth living.'

But I *know* it is not all. How does one know that? Let me take the case of K.M. She has led, ever since she can remember, a very typically false life. Yet, through it all, there have been moments, instants, gleams, when she has felt the possibility of something quite other.

Love-birds at 47*b*: *Male* and female. Male, green underbody, wings mole, tipped with yellow, broad at base, gradually growing smaller until the head feathers, as close as can be. Yellow faces: a touch of pale-blue on the chops and on the top of the beak. On the male exquisite black spots, points of jet under the beak. Tail of male bird blue.

Female yellow with overbody of pale green in delicate pencil lines. The bird is yellow, but a green-yellow. Male bird burrows in its back, finds . . .

September 30. 'Do you know what individuality is?'
'No.'
'Consciousness of will. To be conscious that you have a will and can act.'
Yes, it is. It's a glorious saying.

October 3. Arrived Paris. Took rooms in Select Hotel, Place de la Sorbonne, for ten francs a day per person. What feeling? Very little. The room is like the room where one could work—or so it feels. I have been a perfect torment to L.M. who is pale with dark eyes. I suspect my reactions so much that I hardly dare say what I think of the room and so on. Do I know? Not really. Not more than she.

I have thought of J. to-day. We are no longer together. Am I in the right way, though? No, not yet. Only looking on—telling others. I am not in body and soul. I feel a bit of a sham. . . . And so I am. One of the K.M.'s is so sorry. But of course she is. She has to die. *Don't* feed her.

October. Important. When we can begin to take our failures non-seriously, it means we are ceasing to be afraid of them. It is of immense importance to learn to *laugh at ourselves*. What Shestov calls 'a touch of easy familiarity and derision' has its value.

What will happen to Anatole France and his charming smile? Doesn't it disguise a lack of feeling, like M.'s weariness?

Life should be like a steady, visible light.

What remains of all those years together? It is difficult to say. If they were so important, how could they have come to nothing. Who *gave up* and *why?*

Haven't I been saying, all along, that the fault lies in trying to cure the body and paying no heed whatever to the sick psyche? G. claims to do just what I have always dreamed might be done.

The sound of a street pipe, hundreds and hundreds of years old.

October. The Luxembourg Gardens. A very small railway train came along, with a wooden whistle. First it stopped, blew the whistle, and then moved slowly forward with a wonderfully expressive motion of the right arm. People mattered not at all. It went through them, past them; skirted them. Then down it fell, full length. But two gentlemen picked it up, patted its behind, and in a minute it whistled (rather longer than usual) and started off again. . . .

A little bird-like mother with a baby in her arm, and

tugging at one hand a minute little girl in a coat made out of a pleated skirt, and a pink bow—it looked like pink flannel—on her clubbed hair. A very rich child in a white beaver hat passed and fell quite in love with the pink flannel bow. When its nurse was not looking it hung back and walked beside its little poor sister, looking at her wonderingly and very carefully *keeping step*.

A little person in a pink hat passed, very carefully dragging a minute doll's pram. It was *so* minute she had to drag it on a thread of cotton. Naturally, once she stopped looking and her hand gave a jerk, down fell the pram. For about two minutes she dragged it along on its side. Then she discovered the accident, rushed back, set it up, and looked round very angrily in all directions: *certain* some enemy had knocked it over on purpose. Her little dark direct gaze was quite frightening. Did she see someone?

And then suddenly the wind lifts, and all the leaves, leaves fly forward so gladly, so eagerly, as if they were thankful it is not their turn yet to . . .

October 15. Nietzsche's Birthday. Sat in the Luxembourg Gardens. Cold, wretchedly unhappy. Horrid people at lunch, everything horrid, from *Anfang bis zum Ende*.

October 17. *Laubblätter*. The Four Fountains. The Red Tobacco Plant. English dog. The funeral procession.

Actions and Reactions. The silky husks, like the inside of the paw of a cat. 'Darling'.

Fire is sunlight and returns to the sun again in an unending cycle. . . . G. looks exactly like a desert chief. I kept thinking of Doughty's 'Arabia' . . .

To be wildly enthusiastic, or deadly serious—both are wrong. Both pass. One must keep ever present a sense of humour. It depends entirely on yourself how much you see or hear or understand. But the sense of humour I have found of use in every single occasion of my life. Now perhaps you understand what the word 'indifferent' means. It is to learn not to mind, and not to show your mind.

October 18. In the autumn garden leaves falling. Little footfalls, like gentle whispering. They fly, spin, twirl, shake.

[The following entry was torn out of her journal to be sent to me. But K.M. changed her mind. I found it among her papers with this superscription, 'These pages from my journal. Don't let them distress you. The story *has* a happy ending, really and truly.']

October 10. I have been thinking this morning until it seems I may get things straightened out if I try to write . . . where I am.

Ever since I came to Paris I have been as ill as ever. In fact, yesterday I thought I was dying. It is not imagination. My heart is so exhausted and so tied up that I can only walk to the taxi and back. I get up at midi and go to bed at 5.30. I try to 'work' by fits and starts, but the time has gone by. I cannot work. Ever since April I have done practically nothing. But why? Because, although M.'s treatment improved my blood and made me look well and did have a good effect on my lungs, it made my heart not a snap better, and I only won that improvement by living the life of a corpse in the Victoria Palace Hotel.

My spirit is nearly dead. My spring of life is so starved that it's just not dry. Nearly all my improved health is pretence—acting. What does it amount to? Can I walk? Only creep. Can I do anything with my hands or body? Nothing at all. I am an absolutely help-less invalid. What is my life? It is the existence of a parasite. And five years have passed now, and I am in straighter bonds than ever.

Ah, I feel a little calmer already to be writing. Thank God for writing! I am so terrified of what I am going to do. All the voices out of the 'Past' say 'Don't do it'. J. says 'M. is a scientist. He does his part. It's up to you to do yours.' But that is no good at all. I can no more cure my psyche than my body. Less it seems to me. Isn't J. himself, perfectly fresh and well, utterly depressed by boils on his neck? Think of five years' imprisonment. Someone has got to help me to get out. If that is a confession of weakness—it is. But it's only lack of imagination that calls it so. And who is going to help me? Remember Switzerland: 'I am helpless.' Of course, he is. One prisoner cannot help another. Do I believe in medicine alone? No, never. In science alone?

No, never. It seems to me childish and ridiculous to suppose one can be cured like a cow *if one is not a cow*. And here, all these years, I have been looking for someone who agreed with me. I have heard of G. who seems not only to agree but to know infinitely more about it. Why hesitate?

Fear. Fear of what? Doesn't it come down to fear of losing J.? I believe it does. But, good Heavens! Face things. What have you of him now? What is your relationship? He talks to you—sometimes—and then goes off. He thinks of you tenderly. He dreams of a life with you *some day* when the miracle has happened. You are important to him as a dream. Not as a living reality. For you are not one. What do you share? Almost nothing. Yet there is a deep, sweet, tender flooding of feeling in my heart which is love for him and longing for him. But what is the good of it as things stand? Life together, with me ill, is simply torture with happy moments. But it's not life. . . . You do know that J. and you are only a kind of dream of what might be. And that might-be never, never can be true unless you are well. And you won't get well by 'imagining' or 'waiting' or trying to bring off that miracle yourself.

Therefore if the Grand Lama of Thibet promised to help you—how can you hesitate? Risk! Risk anything! Care no more for the opinions of others, for those voices. Do the hardest thing on earth for you. Act for yourself. Face the truth.

True, Tchehov didn't. Yes, but Tchehov died. And

let us be honest. How much do we know of Tchehov from his letters? Was that all? Of course not. Don't you suppose he had a whole longing life of which there is hardly a word? Then read the final letters. He has given up hope. If you de-sentimentalize those final letters they are terrible. There is no more Tchehov. Illness has swallowed him.

But perhaps to people who are not ill, all this is nonsense. They have never travelled this road. How can they see where I am? All the more reason to go boldly forward alone. Life is not simple. In spite of all we say about the mystery of Life, when we get down to it we want to treat it as though it were a child's tale. . . .

Now, Katherine, what do you mean by health? And what do you want it for?

Answer: By health I mean the power to live a full, adult, living, breathing life in close contact with what I love—the earth and the wonders thereof—the sea—the sun. All that we mean when we speak of the external world. I want to enter into it, to be part of it, to live in it, to learn from it, to lose all that is superficial and acquired in me and to become a conscious direct human being. I want, by understanding myself, to understand others. I want to be all that I am capable of becoming so that I may be (and here I have stopped and waited and waited and it's no good—there's only one phrase that will do) *a child of the sun*. About helping others, about carrying a light and so on, it seems false to say a single word. Let it be at that. *A child of the sun.*

Then I want to *work*. At what? I want so to live that I work with my hands and my feeling and my brain. I want a garden, a small house, grass, animals, books, pictures, music. And out of this, the expression of this, I want to be writing. (Though I may write about cabmen. That's no matter.)

But warm, eager, living life—to be rooted in life—to learn, to desire to know, to feel, to think, to act. That is what I want. And nothing less. That is what I must try for.

———

I wrote this for myself. I shall now risk sending it to J. He may do with it what he likes. He must see how much I love him.

And when I say 'I fear'—don't let it disturb you, dearest heart. We all fear when we are in waiting-rooms. Yet we must pass beyond them, and if the other can keep calm, it is all the help we can give each other. . . .

And this all sounds very strenuous and serious. But now that I have wrestled with it, it's no longer so. I feel happy—deep down. *All is well*.

[With those words Katherine Mansfield's Journal comes to a fitting close. Thenceforward the conviction that 'All was well' never left her. She entered a kind of spiritual brotherhood at Fontainebleau. The object of this brotherhood, at least as she understood it, was to help its members to achieve a spiritual regeneration.

After some three months, at the beginning of 1923, she invited me to stay with her for a week. I arrived early in the afternoon of

January 9. I have never seen, nor shall I ever see, anyone so beautiful as she was on that day; it was as though the exquisite perfection which was always hers had taken possession of her completely. To use her own words, the last grain of 'sediment', the last 'traces of earthly degradation', were departed for ever. But she had lost her life to save it.

As she came up the stairs to her room at 10 p.m. she was seized by a fit of coughing which culminated in a violent hæmorrhage. At 10.30 she was dead.]

THIS EDITION IS COMPOSED IN
OLD FACE STANDARD TYPE CUT BY
THE MONOTYPE CORPORATION.
THE PAPER IS MADE BY THE PAPIER-
FABRIK BAUTZEN. THE PRINTING AND
THE BINDING ARE THE WORK OF
OSCAR BRANDSTETTER · ABTEILUNG
JAKOB HEGNER · LEIPZIG

THE ALBATROSS

MODERN CONTINENTAL LIBRARY

4 new volumes published monthly